CONTENTS

Bering Sea

GULF OF ALASKA

Labrador Sea

Greenland Sea

PACIFIC OCEAN

GULF OF MEXICO

Caribbean Sea

ATLANTIC OCEAN

GULF OF GUIN

ANTARCTI

N

W   E

S

2

...IC SEA

Barents Sea

Norwegian Sea

North Sea

Baltic Sea

East Siberian Sea

Mediterranean Sea

Black Sea

Caspian Sea

Persian Gulf

Red Sea

Arabian Sea

Bering Sea

Sea of Japan

East China Sea

South China Sea

Philippine Sea

BAY OF BENGAL

INDIAN OCEAN

PACIFIC OCEAN

...CEAN

Tasman Sea

WATER ON EARTH

71% water

Earth is covered largely by water: oceans, lakes and rivers make up 71% of the earth's surface. For this reason, when we view our planet from Space, it looks like a large blue ball. In this book we will explore the oceans and seas and their different characteristics, which are a fundamental resource for life on Earth.

WHEN DID THE SEAS AND OCEANS FORM?

The vast amount of water that today makes up the seas and oceans formed over the course of **geologic eras**. Its origin is not known for certain, but one of the soundest theories connects it to the gradual **cooling** of the earth. In fact, originally our planet was covered in incandescent gases and vapours, which escaped from the earth's crust and volcanoes. As the earth cooled, these gasses and vapours condensed, turning into water and falling to the ground, which created the first great ocean: the **Panthalassa**.

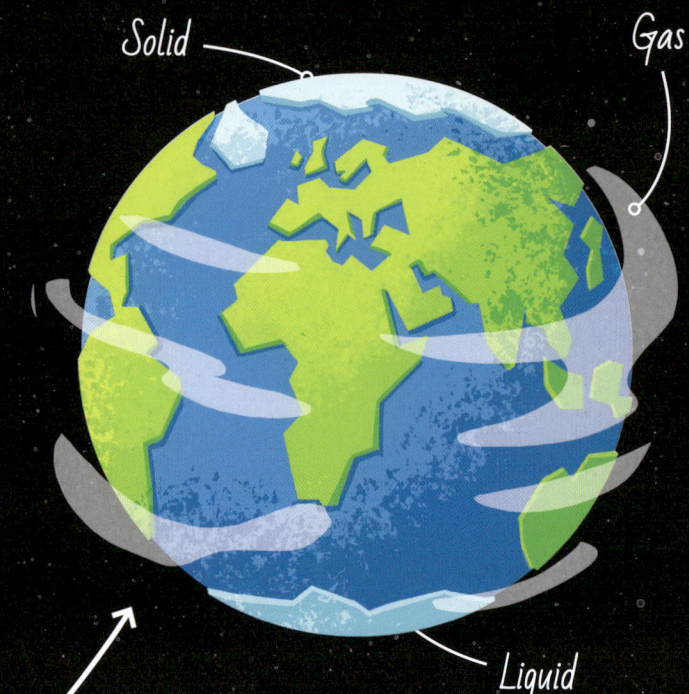

Solid

Gas

Liquid

Pangea

Panthalassa

DID YOU KNOW?

Earth is one of a kind. It is the only planet in our solar system where the average temperature allows water to exist in all three states: **solid**, **liquid** and **gas**.

WHAT IS THE OCEANIC CRUST?

Unlike the continental crust, oceanic crust is thinner, denser and younger. When **oceanic plates** separate, magma escapes from the mantle (the earth's super-solid mass located between the oceanic crust and the earth's superhot core). The escaping mantle forms the **ridges** of underwater mountain ranges. When the oceanic plates collide, on the other hand, the cooler one 'subducts', or descends, beneath the other, creating a depression, known as a **'trench'**.

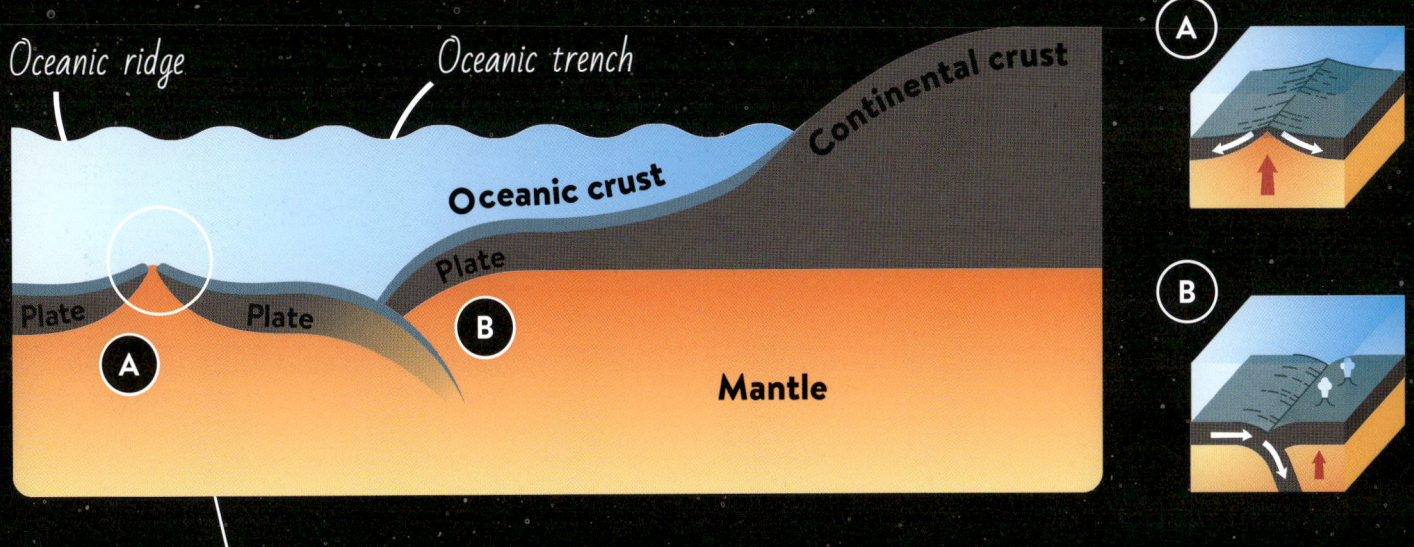

Oceanic ridge

Oceanic trench

Continental crust

Oceanic crust

Plate

Plate

A

Plate

B

Mantle

A

B

① **ZONE 1**
This is the most **superficial** layer, formed from sea sediment, and can vary in composition and thickness.

② **ZONE 2 (volcanic layer)**
This **intermediate** layer consists mainly of basalt, a black volcanic rock.

③ **ZONE 3 (oceanic layer)**
This is the **deepest** layer and is mainly composed of gabbros, igneous rocks with a granular structure.

HOW IS WATER DISTRIBUTED ON EARTH?

Water covers most of the **Southern Hemisphere**, while more of the Northern Hemisphere is covered in land. This means that in the Southern Hemisphere, especially in the temperate zones, the summer and winter temperatures are controlled only by the oceans, so are very similar. In the Northern Hemisphere, by contrary, there is a greater difference between the hot and cold temperatures, because these are influenced by both the oceanic expanses and the emerged lands.

Atlantic Ocean

Mediterranean Sea

Arctic Ocean

NORTHERN

Pacific Ocean

Atlantic Ocean

SOUTHERN

Antarctic Ocean

WHAT IS THE DIFFERENCE BETWEEN A SEA AND AN OCEAN?

Seas and oceans are not the same. Of course both are made up of salt water, but they have major differences that set them apart, so the words are not interchangeable. Seas are smaller than oceans, partially enclosed between strips of land and located where land and ocean meet. Oceans, on the other hand, are boundless expanses of salt water. The earth, in fact, is covered by a single '**world ocean**', which by convention has been divided into five oceans: **Pacific** (the largest), **Atlantic**, **Antarctic**, **Arctic** and **Indian**.

＊ CAN A SEA BECOME AN OCEAN?

There is a sea that over time has been expanding. This is the **Red Sea**, located in Egypt, which gets its name not from its intense green colour but from red algae, which give the sea also a brownish-red colour. That is the theory of its name, at least. One thing is for certain: the Red Sea is destined to become the **sixth ocean** of our planet!

Red Sea

HEMISPHERE

Indian Ocean

HEMISPHERE

○ NOT JUST SEAS...

Do you think salt water is to be found only in seas and oceans? Oh no! Between Jordan and Israel is the **Dead Sea**: the saltiest natural lake in the world. Imagine, the Dead Sea's surface waters are **eight times saltier** than the ocean, and this concentration of salt only increases as you go deeper. Only bacteria can survive in this lake: no other living being can. That's why it's called 'dead'!

Dead Sea

You can try to swim in the Dead Sea, but you will also be able to float very easily!

THE WATER CYCLE

CONDENSATION

This process of transforming water from a gaseous to a **liquid state** happens when the air cools or when air at different temperatures meet.

SUBLIMATION

This happens when **snow and ice** transform into water vapour without first melting into water.

RAINFALL

From condensation, the water vapour that is present in the atmosphere is then released as 'precipitation' in the form of rain or snow, depending on the temperature.

MELTING GLACIERS

LAKE

PERCOLATION

Through this process, precipitation enters into the ground to become part of and feed the **underground water flows**.

Seas and oceans, along with lakes, glaciers, rivers and groundwater, are water reservoirs. Groundwater circulates throughout the water reservoirs, giving life to the 'water cycle' which is powered by the sun's energy.

EVAPORATION

A main processes of the water cycle, during this phase, water transforms from a liquid to a **gas**, that is, it turns into vapour. Water from the ocean, therefore, reaches the atmosphere in the form of water vapour.

TRANSPIRATION

Some precipitation is intercepted and absorbed by trees and vegetation. This water travels through the plants and transforms into (and is released as) **water vapour**.

GROUNDWATER

Groundwater flows much more slowly than surface waters, transporting water from the subsoil towards the seas and oceans.

OCEAN

MARINE ECOSYSTEM

The marine ecosystem, which includes both living organisms and non-living elements, is truly immense and is the largest in the biosphere. This environment is richly diverse and encompasses different minor ecosystems, which are all interconnected. The waters of the seas and oceans, all in close communication, have very similar properties, and for this reason we can consider them as a single large 'biota', even if animals and plants vary from area to area.

WHAT IS A BIOTA?

A biota is all the living organisms, both animals and plants, that live in a specific space within an ecosystem.

WHAT IS A MARINE BIOTA?

A marine biota includes the living organisms that populate both the **pelagic zone** (the open sea), such as plankton and nekton, and the **benthic zone** (the seabed), such as benthos. Some of these organisms may be benthic in one phase of their life and pelagic in another. On the next page, we will discover what these categories of organisms are.

WHICH ORGANISMS FORM PART OF THE MARINE ECOSYSTEM?

The marine ecosystem includes three different groups of organisms: **plankton**, **nekton** and **benthos**.

PLANKTON

These are **microscopic plant and animal organisms** that can live both on the surface and at depth, completely dependent on the movements of the water. They are a vital part of the marine environment food chain, because both nekton and benthos feed on them. Furthermore, the balance of our atmosphere depends greatly on the photosynthesis activities of certain plankton.

NEKTON

These organisms can move independently (such as fish or cetaceans). This group mainly includes vertebrates, molluscs and crustaceans. They can be found at all depths and latitudes, though the greatest variety of nekton is found in tropical waters, where a large number of fish species live.

BENTHOS

These organisms **live on the seafloor**, in the surface sediment and in deeper waters. Benthic organisms are classified according to their size: they range from macro-benthos, greater than a millimetre in size, to micro-benthos, which are smaller in size.

ARE LIVING ORGANISMS DISTRIBUTED EVENLY THROUGHOUT THE MARINE ECOSYSTEM?

No. In fact, based on the characteristics of a given marine environment, different **habitats** are created, each of them populated by particular organisms. These habitats are affected by the depth of the water, the proximity to land, topography and, above all, the **availability of light**: the greater the depth of the water, the less light is able to penetrate, down to depths where light cannot not reach.

LIGHT ZONE AND DARK ZONE

In the Atlantic Ocean is a 'field' of hydrothermal vents known as the **Lost City**. This hydrothermal system is found near the mid-Atlantic Ridge and a transform fault (where two plates meet horizontally). Scientists think that the regions of the ocean floor capable of hosting hydrothermal vents must be far vaster than they had imagined!

WHERE IS LIFE MOST CONCENTRATED IN THE DEEPER DEPTHS?

Around the **hydrothermal vents**, hot water escapes from fractures in the seafloor. These vents are found near oceanic ridges or in volcanic areas. Sunlight does not reach this far down, so living beings cannot feed themselves through photosynthesis. Nor can they find organic sustenance that comes from the surface, because by the time this material reaches the seabed, it has lost all nutrients. Instead, these creatures feed off of specialized **bacteria** that produce energy through **chemosynthesis**, that is, the chemical oxidation of certain inorganic compounds, such as methane, produced by the vents.

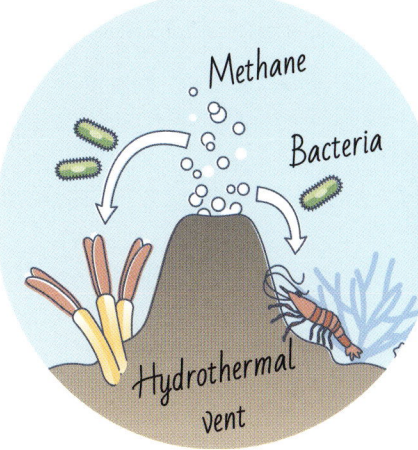

Chemosynthesis

PHOTIC ZONE

Euphotic zone

Disphotic zone

0 m

80 m (262 ft)

200 m (656 ft)

The **photic zone** is the upper layer of the ocean, the layer that receives sunlight. It is actually divided into two zones: the **euphotic zone**, where sunlight allows for the photosynthesis of plants and phytoplankton, and the **disphotic zone**, where the amount of light is not enough for photosynthesis but enough for life for organisms that breathe.

The depths of these areas vary depending on the sunlight, the season, the latitude and the 'turbidity' (clarity) of the water.

APHOTIC ZONE

> 10,000 m (32,808 ft)

Most of the ocean, however, consists of an immense dark region, the **aphotic zone**. Despite the darkness, different organisms can live here. Some of them migrate to the photic zone during the night. Others, such as certain species of sea cucumber or the tripod fish, prefer to remain in the dark for life.

Sea cucumber

Tripod fish

MARINE ZONES AND THEIR DEPTHS

EPIPELAGIC ZONE
0-200 m (0–656 ft)

MESOPELAGIC ZONE
200-1,000 m (656–3,280 ft)

BATHYPELAGIC ZONE
1,000-4,000 m (3,280–13,123 ft)

ABYSSOPELAGIC ZONE
4,000-6,000 m (13,123–19,685 ft)

ADOPELAGIC ZONE
> 6,000 m (> 19,685 ft)

Sea level

0 m

1,000 m
(3,280 ft)

2,000 m
(6,560 ft)

3,000 m
(9,842 ft)

4,000 m
(13,123 ft)

5,000 m
(16,404 ft)

6,000 m
(19,685 ft)

7,000 m
(22,966 ft)

8,000 m
(26,247 ft)

9,000 m
(29,528 ft)

10,000 m
(32,808 ft)

11,000 m
(36,089 ft)

Oceanic trench

The seas, and especially the oceans, are vast expanses of water that hide many secrets. In order to better study this immense **ecosystem**, scientists have divided it into **different zones**, each of which has specific characteristics. The zones they have identified are: the epipelagic zone, the mesopelagic zone, the bathypelagic zone, the abyssopelagic zone and a fifth zone, which is found only in some parts of the world, called the hadopelagic zone.

Coastline

Seafloor

EPIPELAGIC ZONE

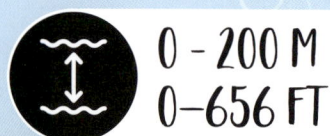

0 - 200 M
0 - 656 FT

The epipelagic zone is also known as the upper ocean zone, the surface of the sea or ocean, where sunlight can reach so photosynthesis can occur. This is why the epipelagic zone is also known as the 'photic', or sunlight, zone! This zone can reach a depth of 200 metres: the clearer the water, the deeper the epipelagic zone. This zone is full of life: in fact, many more creatures live here than in the deeper depths.

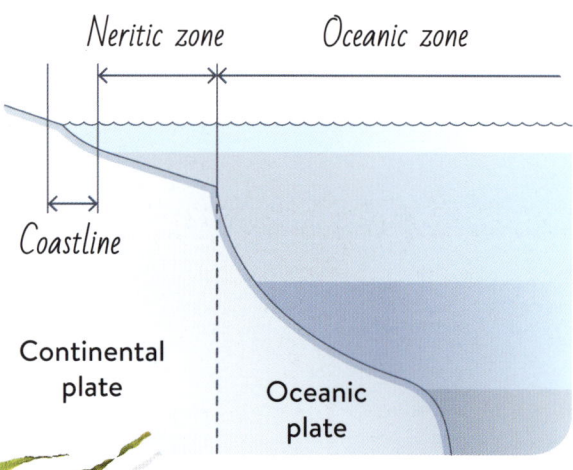

Neritic zone   Oceanic zone

Coastline

Continental plate

Oceanic plate

IS THE EPIPELAGIC ZONE COMPOSED OF ONLY ONE LAYER?

In reality, no: it is divided into a **neritic** epipelagic zone and an **oceanic** epipelagic zone. The neritic zone corresponds to the ocean layer above the continental plate. The oceanic zone corresponds to the surface layer of the ocean above the oceanic plate, that is, the open sea.

WHAT CREATURES LIVE IN THIS ZONE?

All the most well-known marine creatures live here: cetaceans, such as dolphins and whales, species of jellyfish, sharks, sea turtles and plankton. Here, because of the sunlight, many **algae** grow, producing food needed by the entire ocean and also, thanks to **photosynthesis**, 50% of the oxygen that exists in the atmosphere. The organisms that live in this zone can come into contact with organisms that inhabit the coast.

IS THIS ZONE A WELCOMING PLACE?

Not always. The organisms that inhabit the coast are subject to the movements of the waves, the forces of the wind, varying pressure, temperature changes and the distribution of prey. This zone, in fact, is vast, and the creatures that live here often have to **travel long distances** to feed. The same is also true for reproduction. Moreover, organisms already at the mercy of the currents also have to deal with the presence of humans, who navigate the waters, explore and fish.

Blue-ringed octopus

MULTICOLOURED CREATURES

In the epipelagic zone, 40 to 60 metres below the surface, especially in tropical areas where the water has a temperature between 18° and 30° C (65° and 86° F), truly extraordinary living organisms thrive: **coral reefs**. These reefs are made up of corals and madrepores and host a diversity of fauna: ranging from echinoderms, such as the sunflower sea star or the purple sea urchin, to crustaceans, such as the arrow crab, and molluscs, such as the blue-ringed octopus—not to mention the various multicoloured fish that swim among the corals.

Purple sea urchin

Sunflower sea star

Arrow crab

The longest coral reef is in Australia, and reaches 2,300 km (1,429 mi) in length!

MESOPELAGIC ZONE

200 - 1,000 M
656–3,280 FT

The mesopelagic zone is the area between 200 (656 ft) and 1,000 (3,280 ft) metres deep. Some sunlight reaches here but not enough for photosynthesis: this is why this area is known as the 'twilight zone', located between the epipelagic zone, where the sunlight is strong, and the bathypelagic zone, where darkness reigns. As you descend the depths, the temperatures become lower and lower, while the pressure and salinity of the water increase.

WHAT IS THE THERMOCLINE?

The thermocline is the **transition** layer where **temperatures** change rapidly between the epipelagic zone, where the water is warmer, and the mesopelagic zone, where it is colder. The depth of the thermocline changes every year, depending on the season and the location. In tropical regions it is almost always the same, while in polar regions it is found quite close to the surface. In temperate regions it often changes, usually deeper during the summer.

Epipelagic zone	15° C (59° F)
Thermocline	
Mesopelagic zone	4° C (39° F)

Example of a thermocline

WHAT CREATURES LIVE IN THIS ZONE?

The creatures that live in this zone include jellyfish, eels, squid, shrimps and zooplankton. These animals have adapted to life in this area. Some species have **silver scales** that reflect light, while others have **very developed eyes** directed upwards, useful for locating prey and predators. Still others can generate their own light through a feature known as '**bioluminescence**'.

Part of a swordfish's body is covered with silvery scales that reflect the light coming through the ocean's surface.

WHAT DO THE ORGANISMS IN THE MESOPELAGIC ZONE EAT?

As already noted, **very little light** arrives in this area of the ocean, and consequently all the organisms that need photosynthesis to survive cannot live here. In fact, because of the lack of light, as well as the little oxygen, cold temperatures and high salinity of the water, there are **very few nutritional resources** to be found here. Consequently, the creatures that populate this zone migrate regularly to the epipelagic zone in search of food. They travel mostly when darkness falls to avoid diurnal (daytime) predators.

A VAST FOOD WEB

Many animals of the mesopelagic zone, such as **zooplankton**, for example, feed on **phytoplankton**, most abundant at the surface area, part of the epipelagic zone. Zooplankton is an excellent guide to other creatures of this ocean region: they are, in fact, a source of food for certain organisms of the epipelagic zone, which in turn are food for animals coming from deeper zones. The **bacteria** here are very important because they capture carbon dioxide and transform it into other substances, such as carbohydrates or proteins, essential for marine life.

Phytoplankton: organisms belonging to plankton that carry out photosynthesis.

Zooplankton: animal organisms that do not move autonomously but are carried by the currents.

BATHYPELAGIC ZONE

1,000 - 4,000 M
3,280–13,123 FT

Between the mesopelagic zone and the abyssopelagic zone there is the bathypelagic zone, between 1,000 and 4,000 metres (3,280-13,123 ft) beneath the oceanic surface. Here the sun's rays do not reach, and for this reason it is also known as the 'midnight zone'. The only light present is that produced by the resident creatures through bioluminescence.

WHAT EXACTLY IS BIOLUMINESCENCE?

As we have read, some organisms can produce light through bioluminescence, a phenomenon triggered by the energy released from certain chemical reactions inside the body. These marine organisms use bioluminescence to scare off or avoid predators, to locate and attract prey, and to communicate with members of their species.

WHAT ARE THE TEMPERATURE AND PRESSURE LIKE?

Unlike the areas above, here the **temperature is constant**, always hovering at 4° C (39° F), so at this depth, water is close to freezing. The **pressure** is also considerable, but the animals living here are well able for it, as their bodies are mainly composed of water, so they are not crushed!

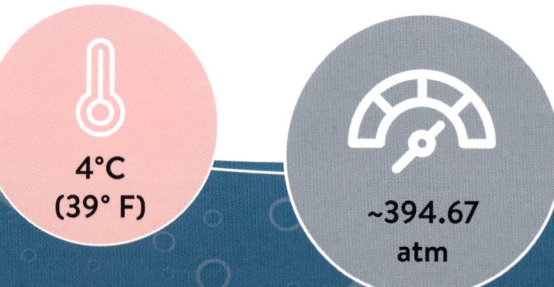

4°C
(39° F)

~394.67
atm

DID YOU KNOW?

When fish from the bathypelagic zone are brought to the surface, their appearance becomes quite bizarre from when they are immersed in water. This is because the surface pressure is much lower than that at depth: their eyes swell and the gases inside their body expand, making them practically **explode**!

HOW DO THEY OBTAIN FOOD?

In the bathypelagic zone, food is even more scarce than in the mesopelagic zone, which is why only a few creatures live here. Furthermore, since these creatures are far from sunlight and have little energy available, they prefer to remain still and wait for prey or attract them with **bioluminescence**. Imagine, most of these creatures measure no more than 10 centimetres, to minimize expending energy.

HOW DO THEY DEFEND THEMSELVES FROM PREDATORS?

The creatures that live here are able to identify predators (and also their own prey!) thanks to highly developed **acoustic systems**. Furthermore, to avoid being detected, unlike the creatures in the upper zones, most of them have **dark colours** and are not covered with silvery scales, which might reflect bioluminescence. Imagine, even the red-coloured fish turn out black, because at depth red light is absent!

Fish that belong to the *Cetomimidae* family have eyes so small and underdeveloped they are unable to focus on images. On the other hand, their bodies are covered with **sensory pores**, which allow them to detect the presence of predators.

To distract predators, fish belonging to the *Platytroctidae* family have an **internal sac**, located at the level of the 'shoulders', containing bioluminescent fluid which when released forms a bright blue cloud.

ABYSSOPELAGIC ZONE

The abyssopelagic zone, also called the abyssal zone, extends from 4,000 (13,123 ft) to 6,000 (19,685 ft) metres deep. Here the darkness is absolute...you can't see a thing! The name of this zone derives from the Greek word ábyssos which means 'bottomless', because it was once thought that the ocean actually had no end. The temperatures here are so low that the water is always close to the freezing point. In this zone also, the waters are very calm, because they are very far from the turbulence at the water's surface that creates the currents and the waves.

Those creatures able to move at these depths are equipped with long legs. Those that remain attached to the seabed are equipped with **peduncles,** which allow them to 'hover' just above the seafloor, where oxygen is almost non-existent.

DID YOU KNOW?

The **pollutants** produced on the earth unfortunately also reach these depths. These include **plastic**, which is particularly harmful to this area because the organisms that live here have evolved to eat anything that moves. Hence, many living beings consume plastic instead of nutrients.

2-3°C
(35.5°–37.4° F)

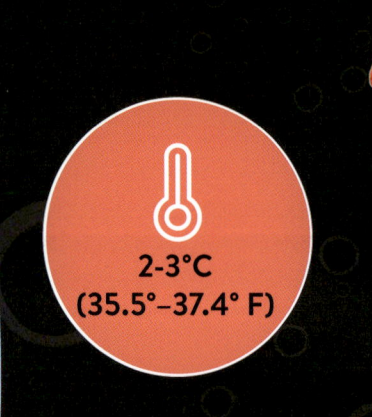

IS THERE OXYGEN?

Despite the profound depths, oxygen is present, although in a much lower quantity than in the surface waters. The abyssal water comes exclusively from **melted polar ice**, and the amount of oxygen present remains equal to what these waters contained before melting. Because of the absence of light, in fact, photosynthesis cannot take place and therefore oxygen cannot be produced.

WHAT ORGANISMS HAVE ADAPTED TO LIVE HERE?

The creatures that have adapted to live in this zone are rare and belong to only a **few species**. There are several marine invertebrates and types of fish that have learned to live in this environment where there is no distinction between day and night or between seasons, where pressure and darkness reign and where the seafloor is formed of soft sediment. Organisms here are mostly grey, black or transparent.

Dumbo octopus

Giant squid

Many fish and crustaceans are blind and, as depth increases, carnivores and scavengers are fewer and fewer, giving way to animals that feed on mud or sediment. These fish often have **huge, wide-open jaws** and **sharp teeth**.

WHAT IS ABYSSAL GIGANTISM?

Abyssal gigantism refers to the phenomenon whereby some species that live in deep waters reach much larger sizes than similar animals that live in more surface waters. Since the abyss is very difficult to study, there is still no established explanations for this phenomenon.

3 m
(9.8 ft)

30 kg
(66 lbs)

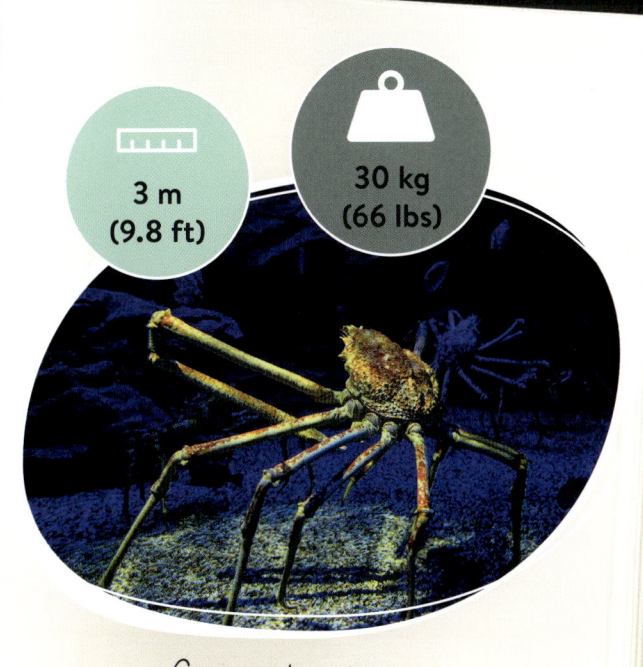

Giant crab of Japan

HADOPELAGIC ZONE

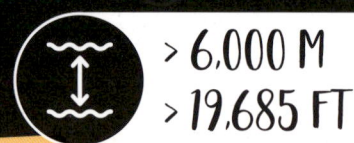

> 6,000 M
> 19,685 FT

The hadopelagic zone is found at depths greater than 6,000 metres (19,685 ft), which are usually reached in ocean trenches and is the lowest layer of the ocean. This zone takes its name from the Greek god of the underworld, Hades, precisely because it is practically impossible to live at these depths, due to the very low temperatures and enormous pressure. This ocean layer is still largely unexplored and only a very few species are known to survive here, most of which live near the hydrothermal vents.

WHAT IS THE DEEPEST POINT OF ALL THE OCEANS?

It is the **Challenger Deep**, located in the Mariana Trench, in the Pacific Ocean. This crescent-shaped pit is about 2,550 km (1,585 mi) long and 69 km (43 mi) wide, and its deepest point is known as the Challenger Deep, which is about **11 km (7 mi) deep**. Imagine, if Mount Everest were placed into the Mariana Trench, there would still be about 2 km (1.3 mi) of water left before reaching the bottom!

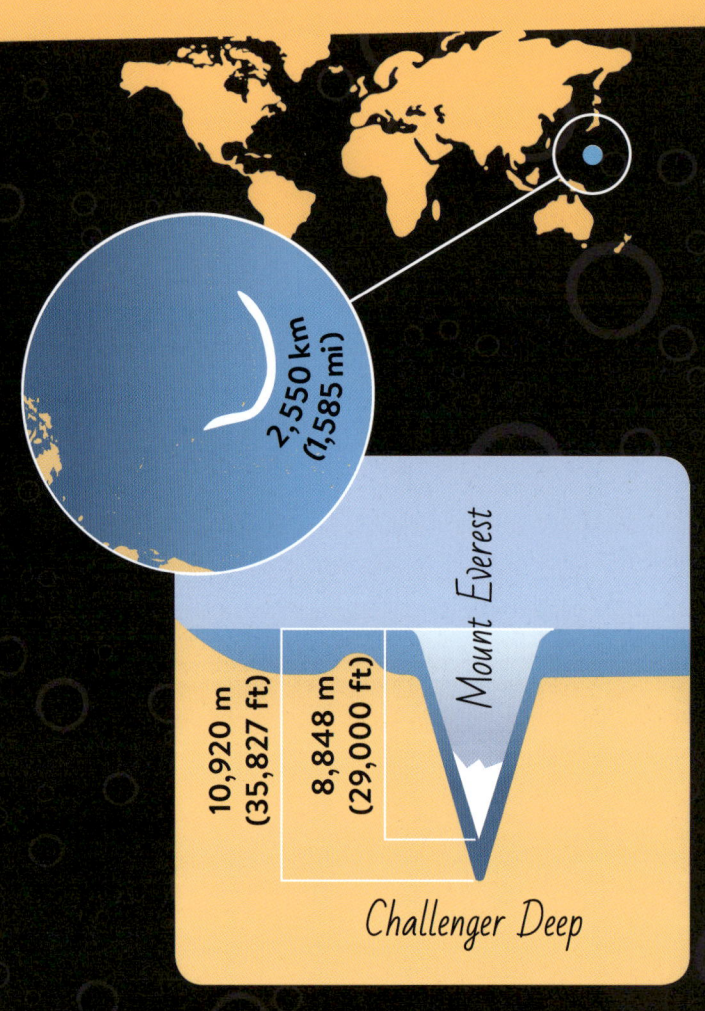

2,550 km (1,585 mi)

10,920 m (35,827 ft)

8,848 m (29,000 ft)

Mount Everest

Challenger Deep

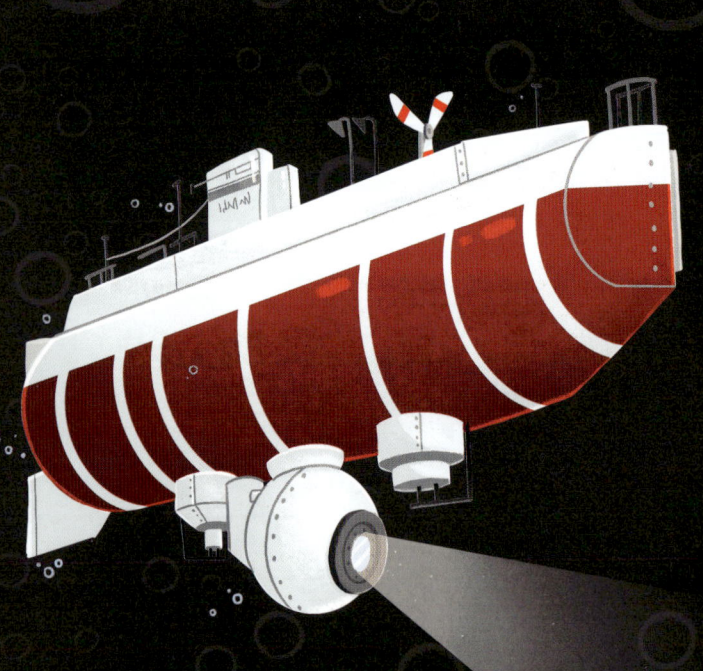

The first humans who reached the Challenger Deep are Jacques Piccard and Don Walsh, in 1960, aboard the Trieste bathyscaphe. Too bad they weren't able to take any photos from inside: the submarine had pushed up clouds of silt that obscured the view!

WHAT ARE THE DEEPEST POINTS OF THE OTHER OCEANS?

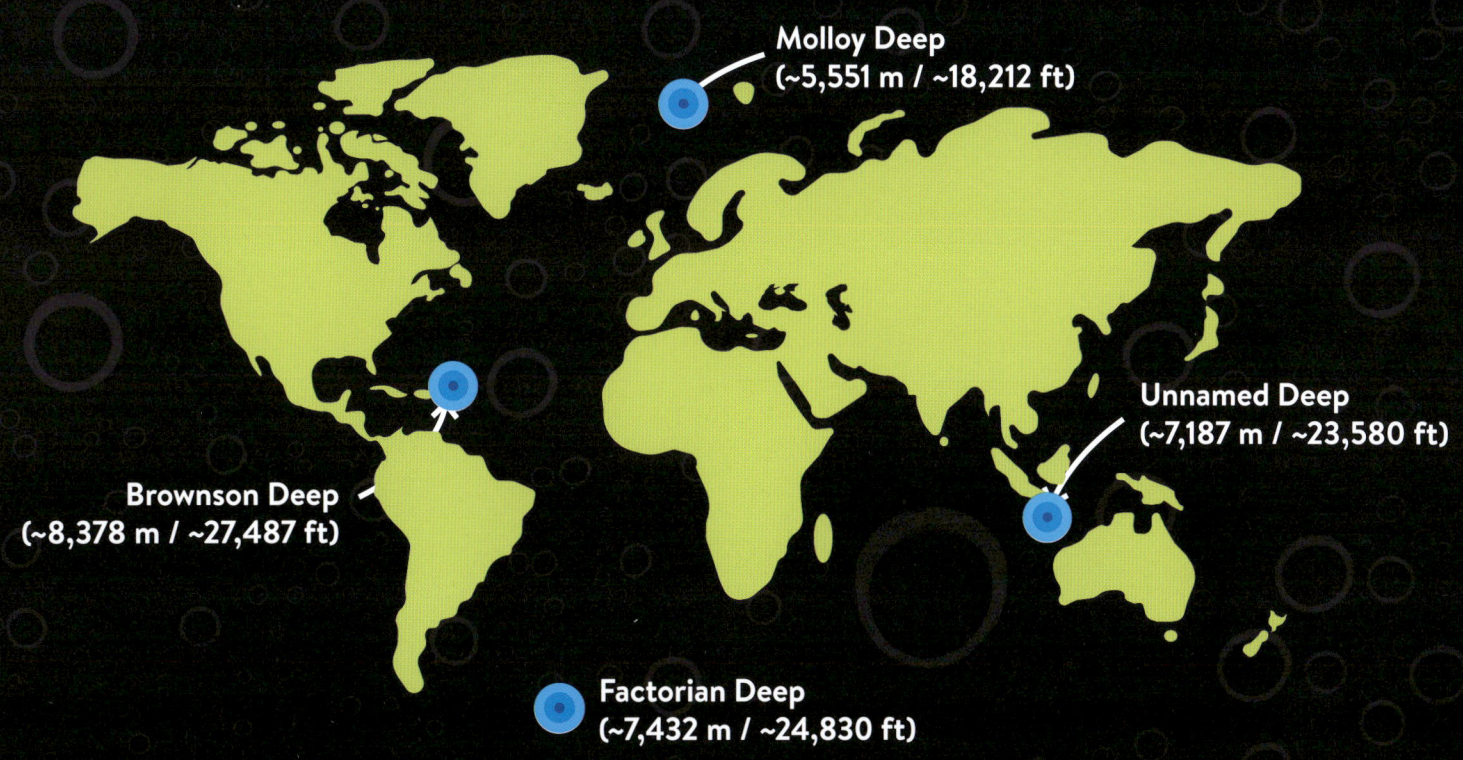

Molloy Deep
(~5,551 m / ~18,212 ft)

Unnamed Deep
(~7,187 m / ~23,580 ft)

Brownson Deep
(~8,378 m / ~27,487 ft)

Factorian Deep
(~7,432 m / ~24,830 ft)

HOW DO WE KNOW THE DEEPEST DEPTHS?

More and more sophisticated instruments are used to measure the ocean depths. Among these are sonar, able to calculate the distance from the seafloor through ultrasound echo. This technique is already present in nature: there are many animals, both terrestrial and marine, that use **ultrasound** and **echolocation** to measure distance and location.

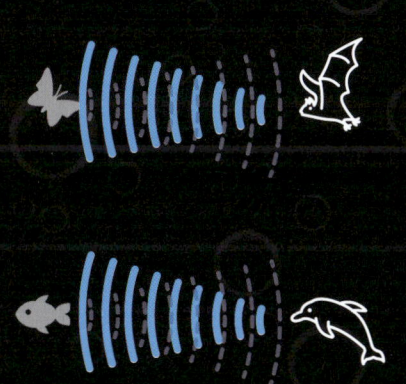

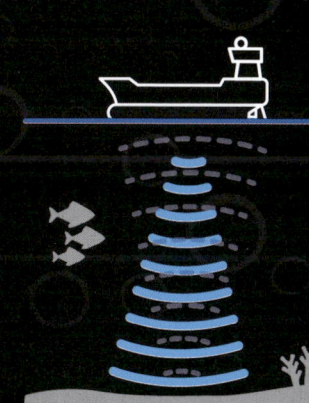

WHAT FISH LIVES AT THE DEEPEST DEPTH?

The **Mariana snailfish**! Imagine, it was spotted 7,900 metres (25,919 feet) below the surface of the ocean. Its shape is like that of a tadpole, though it reaches 20 centimetres (8 inches) long. Its body has no scales and is transparent and gelatinous, which is why it was given the name 'snail'. It feeds on crustaceans, which it sucks in or swallows whole.

THE TIDES

During the day, the levels of the seas and oceans around the world vary, increasing and decreasing. This is the phenomenon of the tides. Each day, on most of Earth, there occur two high tides and two low tides, which are caused by the force of gravity from the Moon and the Sun on our planet.

WHAT IS THE DIFFERENCE BETWEEN LOW AND HIGH TIDE?

Low tide occurs when the water along the coasts moves away from the coast dropping to its minimum height. On the other hand, **high tide** occurs when the sea water moves in towards the coast rising to its maximum height. The time between high tide and low tide is called the '**lunitidal interval**'.

High tide

Low tide

A SPECTACLE OF NATURE

In France there is a place unique in the world specifically because of the alternation of low and high tides, so unique it is considered a **UNESCO World Heritage Site**. The small village of **Le Mont-Saint-Michel** resides on an island made of rock and surrounded by a bay. When the tide is low, you can reach the island on foot, walking on an expanse of sand which is connected to the mainland. At high tide, however, the village becomes a true island, as that expanse becomes submerged underwater.

WHY DOES HIGH TIDE OCCUR ON OPPOSITE SIDES OF THE EARTH?

Earth rotates on its axis, so coastal waters are affected by two different forces. Let's see what these are!

FORCE OF ATTRACTION FROM THE SUN AND THE MOON ON TERRESTRIAL WATERS

Sun

Moon

High tide

Low tide

Low tide

High tide

1

2

1 The Moon exerts its **gravitational pull** on the oceans and seas on the side of Earth facing the Moon, causing a high tide.

2 On the opposite side of Earth, the oceans and seas compensate by 'bulging out' out away from the Moon, also causing a high tide: like the **centrifugal force** you might feel when a car makes a sharp turn in a roundabout. For tides, that force is caused by Earth and the Moon revolving around the Sun.

WHAT ARE TIDE POOLS?

Along the coasts, special **pools** often form among the rocks, which are visible at low tide. These pools host a great variety of animals and plants, which are food for larger species. The presence of these pools is closely related to the movements of the waves, which at times fill them with water and at other times leave them dry.

THE OCEAN CURRENTS

Ocean currents describe the movement of the sea and ocean waters from one place to another. This motion is directional, predictable and continuous, and can be either horizontal or vertical. The system of currents influences changes in biodiversity, Earth's climate and the movements of heat.

WHAT ARE THE THREE MAIN FACTORS AFFECTING OCEAN CURRENTS?

TIDES

The rise and fall of the tides create currents that are stronger in the bays, estuaries and near the coast. These currents are called '**tidal currents**'. The tides change regularly, so these currents are very predictable.

WIND

The wind affects the surface currents. Near the coasts, they cause phenomena such as coastal **upwelling** and coastal **downwelling**. On the other hand, in open water currents allow water to circulate for thousands of kilometres across the ocean basins.

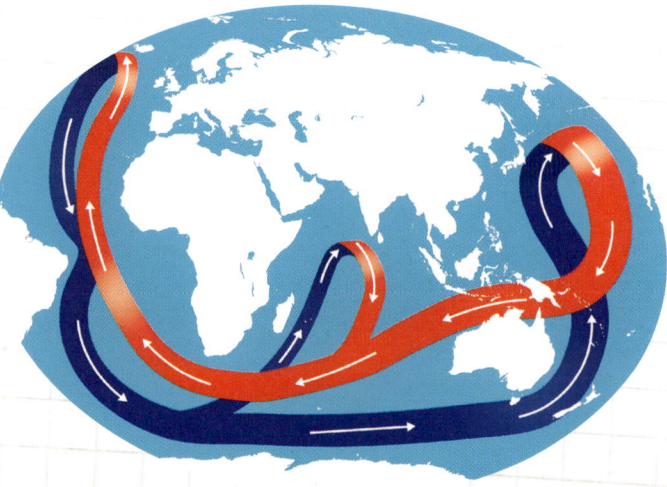

THERMOHALINE CIRCULATION

Thermohaline circulation marks the difference in water density due to changes in **temperature** and **salinity** in different parts of the ocean. Currents affected by thermohaline circulation occur both at depth and more towards the surface, but these currents move more slowly than those caused by the winds and tides.

WHAT IS MEANT BY COASTAL UPWELLING AND DOWNWELLING?

Upwelling is caused when winds blow across the ocean surface pushing water away. Then the water beneath, rich in nutrients, rises up to the surface to replace the water that had been pushed away by the wind.

Downwelling is the reverse, when wind causes surface water to build up along a coastline, forcing the surface water to sink towards the bottom.

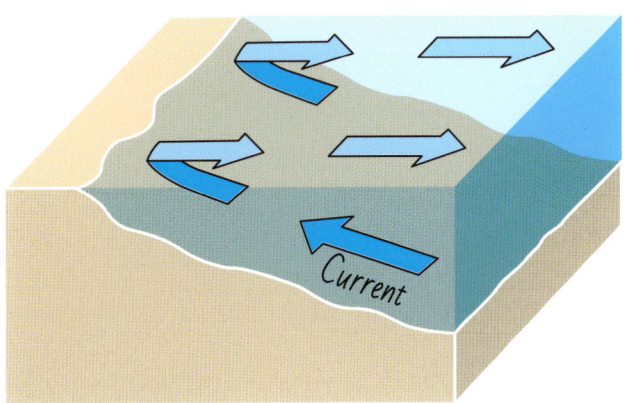

UPWELLING

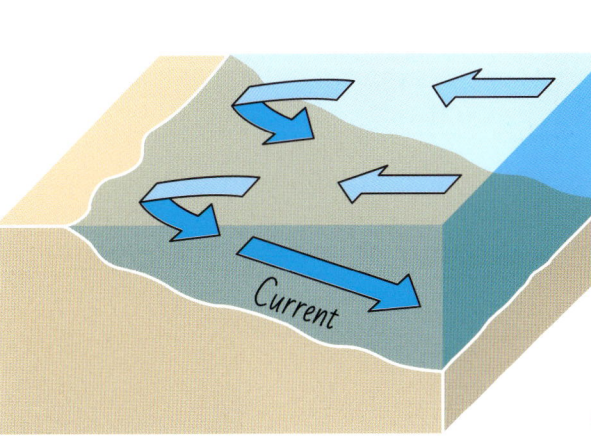

DOWNWELLING

If you get caught in a rip current, to escape you must swim parallel to the beach, to the right or to the left.

WHAT IS A RIP CURRENT?

A rip current is a **strong current** that flows away from the coast towards the open sea or ocean. This current is fast and can reach **8 kilometres (5 miles) per hour.** This makes it very dangerous for swimmers! However, do not confuse it with the undertow current, which pulls swimmers towards the seabed.

Labrador Current
The Labrador Current is a **shallow cold current** that flows south from the Arctic Ocean along the western side of the Labrador Sea. Each year it transports thousands of icebergs. The salinity of the water is low.

Warm currents
Cold currents

Alaskan Current
The Alaskan Current is a surface ocean current, which turns **counter-clockwise** in the Gulf of Alaska. It is a shallow warm-water current with a temperature greater than 4°C (39.2°F).

Gulf Stream
The Gulf Stream is a powerful ocean current that carries **warm water** from the Gulf of Mexico to the Atlantic Ocean, along the entire east coast of the United States and Canada, reaching as far as Western Europe.

Antarctic Circumpolar Current
This is an ocean current that flows clockwise from west to east, driven by the wind that surrounds Antarctica. It is an **irregular current** in both its course and its width, because it is effected by the winds, the underwater topography and the nearby water masses.

THE MAJOR CURRENTS

Kuroshio

The Kuroshio current plays an important role in **warming** the coastal regions of southern and south-eastern Japan, as far as Tokyo. Its flow varies according to the seasons: from May to August it is strongest, recedes in the fall, increases from January to February and then weakens again in the spring.

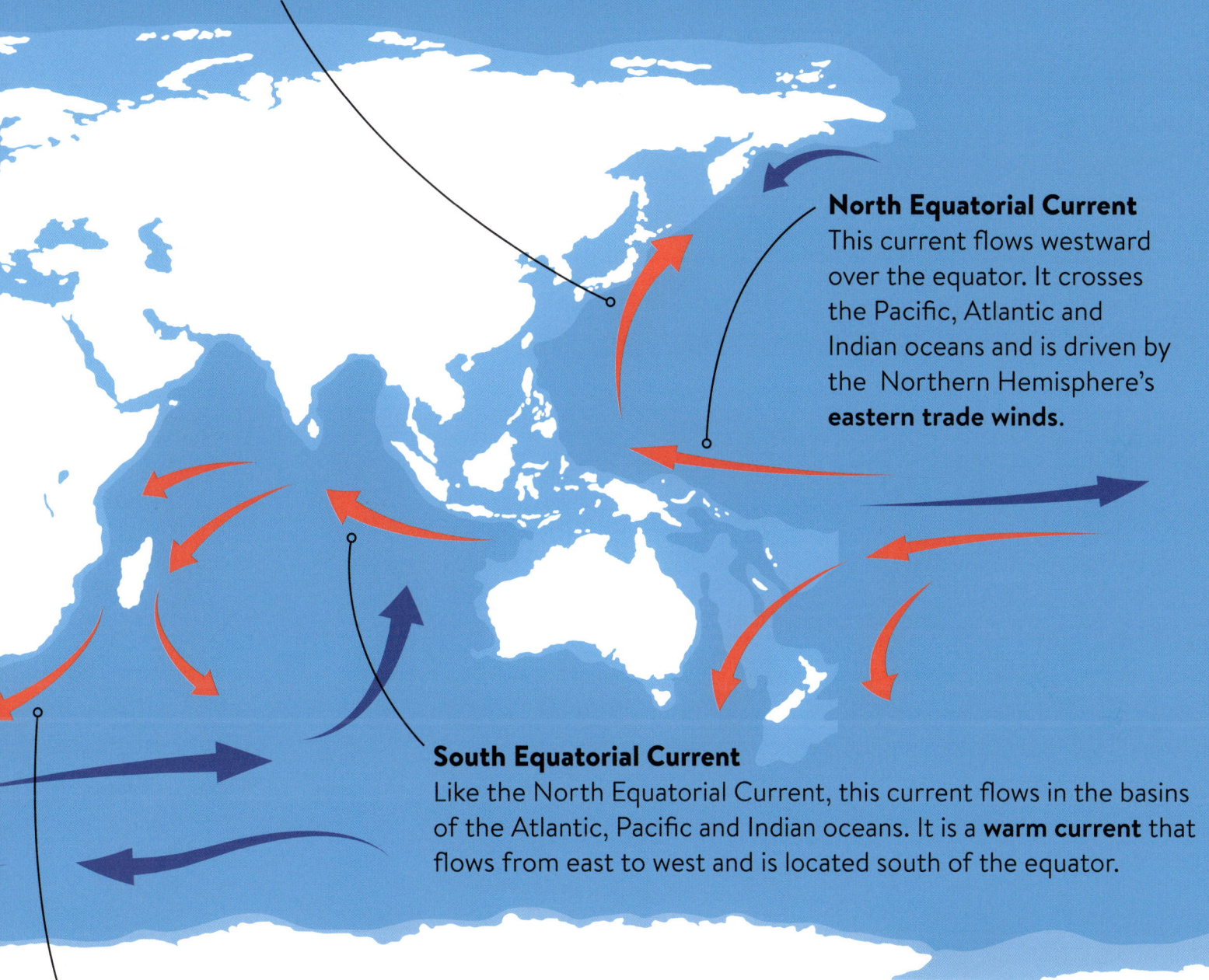

North Equatorial Current

This current flows westward over the equator. It crosses the Pacific, Atlantic and Indian oceans and is driven by the Northern Hemisphere's **eastern trade winds**.

South Equatorial Current

Like the North Equatorial Current, this current flows in the basins of the Atlantic, Pacific and Indian oceans. It is a **warm current** that flows from east to west and is located south of the equator.

Mozambique Current

This is a relatively warm surface current, located in the western Indian Ocean. It greatly influences the climate of the **island of Madagascar** as well as the African mainland. To the south of Madagascar, it travels with the South Equatorial Current into the Agulhas Current.

In this picture you can see the major ocean currents of the world.

CLIMATE AND CURRENTS

The seas and oceans play a fundamental role in Earth's climate. Most of the Sun's radiation, in fact, is absorbed by the waters, especially around the equator.

Seas and oceans help **distribute heat** on the planet: sea water evaporates constantly, causing temperatures and humidity to rise to form storms and rains, which are carried by the trade winds to the land. In all of this, ocean currents play a very important role.

WHAT EFFECTS DOES CLIMATE CHANGE HAVE ON CURRENTS?

The world's major currents are slowing because of **global warming**. The rise in temperatures is causing the glaciers to melt, which in turn cause the fresh water from the melted ice to mix with the ocean's surface, decreasing the salinity of the ocean water, resulting in a **slower flow.** This could lead to the complete blocking of the global currents which would cause severe **climate changes** worldwide.

°C °F
50 120
40 100
30 80
20 60
10 40
0
10 20
20 0
30 20

WHY ARE CURRENTS IMPORTANT FOR THE CLIMATE?

The currents cause thermohaline circulation, also known as the **Great Conveyor Belt**, which carries warm water and precipitation from the equator towards the Poles, and cold water from the Poles towards the tropics. This flow of currents is divided into **5 phases**. Currents regulate Earth's climate, which would otherwise be irregular given that solar radiation reaches Earth unevenly. Without the currents, temperatures would be extreme, freezing cold at the Poles and boiling hot at the equator.

The dense, salty, cold water of the northern polar regions sinks and travels south into the Atlantic Ocean.

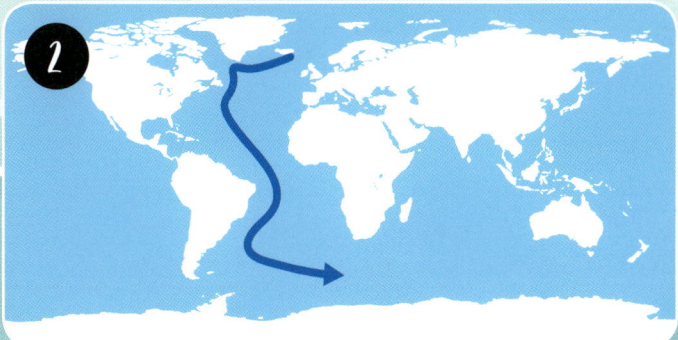

On the way, when it passes near Antarctica, the current 'recharges' with more dense, cold, salty water.

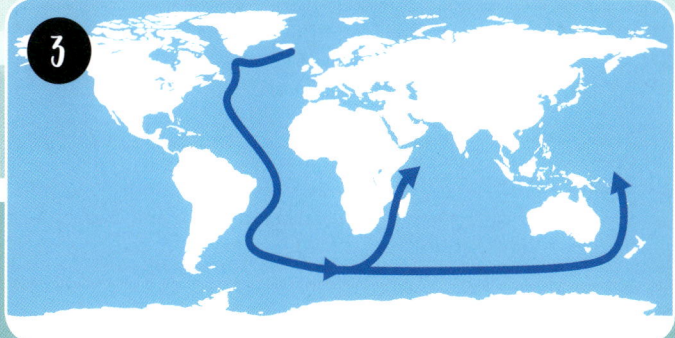

The current splits in two: one travels towards the western Pacific Ocean, while the other towards the Indian Ocean.

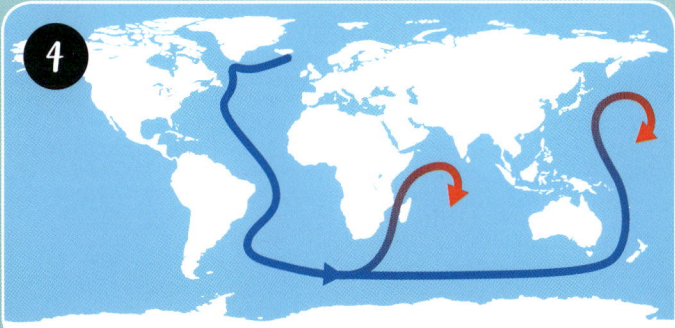

These two currents warm up as they head north, then return back, west and south.

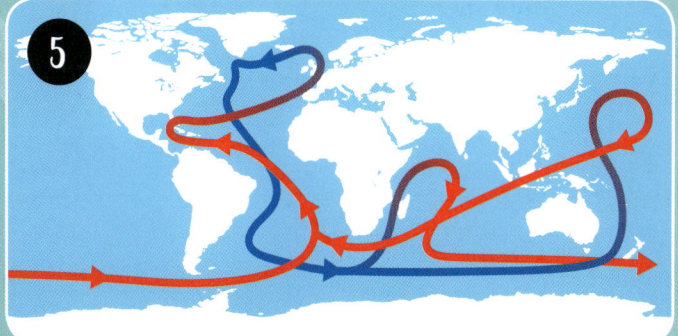

Therefore, the surface waters warm up and circulate around the earth, and then return to the North Atlantic and start the cycle again.

WAVES

When you go to the beach, whether the sea or the ocean, one of the main features is the breaking of the waves on the shore. Some love to ride the waves on a surfboard. Others prefer to be lulled by the currents while lying on a raft. Still others enjoy diving in head first! The immense expanses of water may at times appear calm, but the water is actually in constant motion. So, what are waves?

HOW DO WAVES FORM?

Waves are formed by **energy**, usually generated by the wind, which create friction with the water. The wind passes through the water making it move circularly. You might think that waves move the water from one place to another, but not so! A wave rises and then returns to the sea to the same location. Just watch an object being lifted and then dropped by the waves: the waves raise it and drop it at the same spot! Waves follow one after the other, creating **wave motion**.

WHAT ARE THE DIFFERENT PARTS OF A WAVE?

FREQUENCY
Number of crests that pass **point A** every second

PERIOD
Time it takes the crest at **point A** to reach **point B**

Wind

Length

A   B

Height

Crest

Level of calm sea

Trough

Sea current

Water's edge

ARE ALL WAVES THE SAME?

No, they differ according to the **energy source** that generates them.

SURFACE WAVES

These waves are normally seen from the beach, which ripple the surface of the water, both in the open sea and near the shore. They are generated by the **wind**: the stronger, faster and longer the wind, the larger the waves become. The waves' height depends on these factors.

STORM WAVES

These are **potentially dangerous waves** and are caused by powerful storms that form inland, such as hurricanes. These are not the waves we usually see, but they cause a sharp rise in the sea level that reaches the shore and can destroy coastal environments. So these waves form offshore in **deep water**, and intensify as they approach the coast.

TSUNAMI

These are gigantic waves caused by **landslides**, **volcanic eruptions** or **underwater earthquakes**, which move large quantities of water very quickly, creating very long waves. Like storm waves, tsunamis can also be extremely dangerous, as they destroy everything in their path when they reach the coast.

TSUNAMIS

As we have read, tsunamis are truly catastrophic waves. They are formed by a series of very long waves, which travel out in all directions from the point of origin, like the ripples caused by throwing a stone into a body of water. Let's find out more!

800 km/h (497 mph)

HOW DO TSUNAMIS MOVE IN THE OCEANS?

In deep water tsunamis travel at exorbitant speeds. They can reach **800 km/h (497 mph)**, the same speed as an airplane. They slow down as the sea depth decreases.

HOW DO THE LENGTH, PERIOD AND HEIGHT OF TSUNAMI WAVES CHANGE?

The length and period of the waves depend on the triggering event. If the tsunami is caused by a landslide, the wavelength and period will be shorter. On the other hand, if the wave is generated by a powerful earthquake, the length and period will be greater. Usually, the wave period varies from **5 to 90 minutes**, and the length can range **from a few to hundreds of kilometres/miles**. As the tsunami waves approach the coast, the wave length decreases and the wave height increases. In deep water, from where the tsunami wave travels, the wave height can range between only a few centimetres/inches and just over a metre (3 feet).

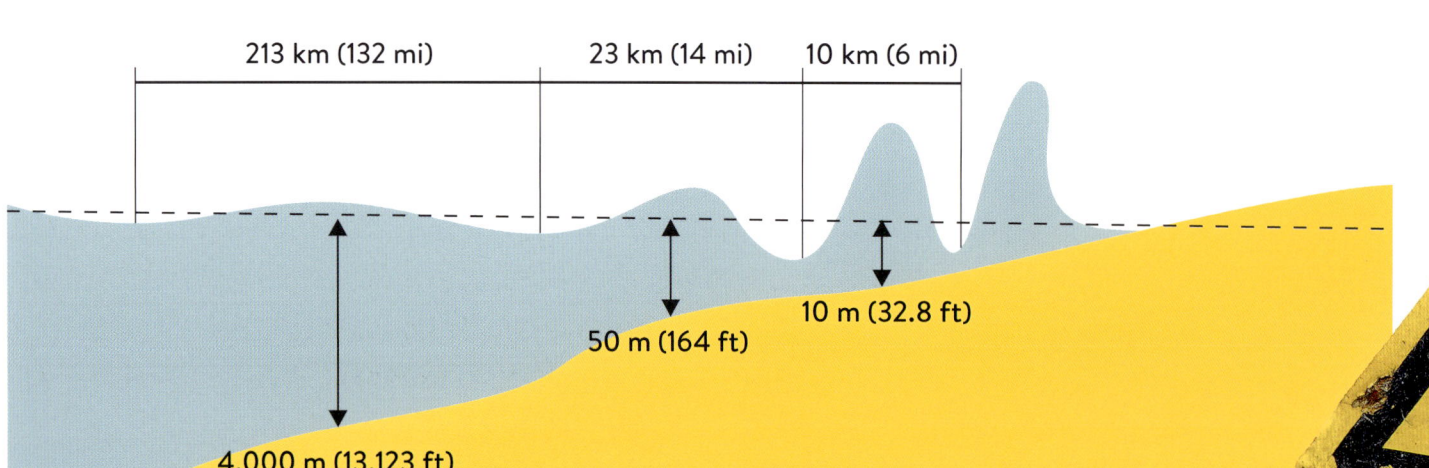

213 km (132 mi)   23 km (14 mi)   10 km (6 mi)

50 m (164 ft)

10 m (32.8 ft)

4,000 m (13,123 ft)

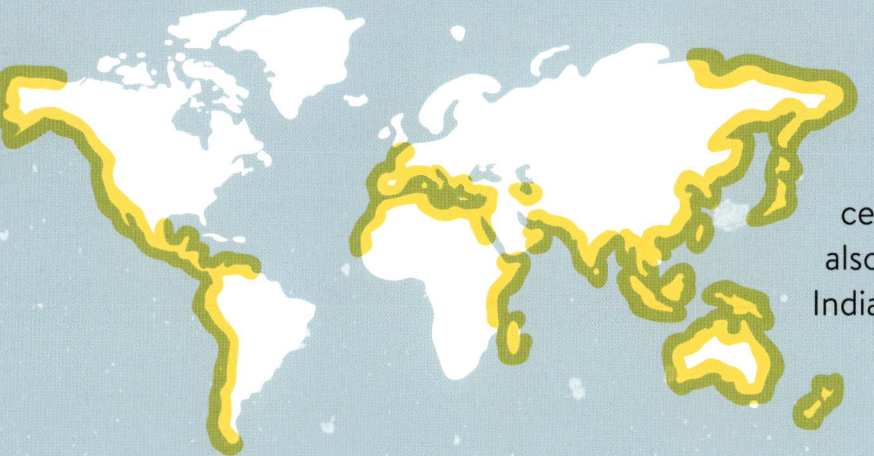

WHERE DO TSUNAMIS OCCUR?

The most active region for tsunamis is the **Pacific Ocean**, but over the centuries devastating tsunamis have also occurred in the Atlantic Ocean and Indian Ocean, in the Caribbean Sea and even in the Mediterranean Sea.

WHAT ARE SOME OF THE MOST DEVASTATING TSUNAMIS?

The most devastating tsunami ever recorded to date occurred in 2004 in the **Indian Ocean**, near the coast of Sumatra, Indonesia: a 9.0 magnitude earthquake and the movement of the tectonic plates displaced a vast amount of water, which hit and destroyed the coasts of Thailand, India, Sri Lanka and Indonesia, reaching as far as East Africa. The devastation caused 230,000 deaths and extensive damage to infrastructures.

In 2011, there was a particularly strong tsunami in **Japan**, which caused damage to settlements and the environment, as well as almost 16,000 deaths.

230,000
casualties

© shutterstock / Frans Delian

Indonesia, 2004

ARE THERE SIGNS THAT A TSUNAMI IS APPROACHING?

Along the coasts of the Pacific Ocean, where most tsunamis occur, **warning systems** have been set up to detect major earthquakes, **of magnitude 7.0 or greater**, and unusual changes in sea level. This alarm system is able to warn people living in coastal areas of the arrival of a tsunami, allowing them to **evacuate** in time.

SEA FAUNA

WHAT ARE THE SHARED TRAITS OF FISH?

Fish are vertebrates. That is, they have a backbone. They breathe underwater with their **gills**, have fins and scales and lay eggs. They are **cold-blooded**, so their body temperature depends on the water in which they live. They can be divided into cartilaginous fish and bony fish.

ANATOMY OF A FISH

MOUTH

The form of a fish's mouth depends on the food it eats and its habitat. Some reef species have small mouths (for sucking) and some have strong beaks. Predators have sharp teeth and jaws with a very broad opening. Deep-sea fish have giant mouths with sharp teeth, or suction-like mouths that suck in nourishmenti.

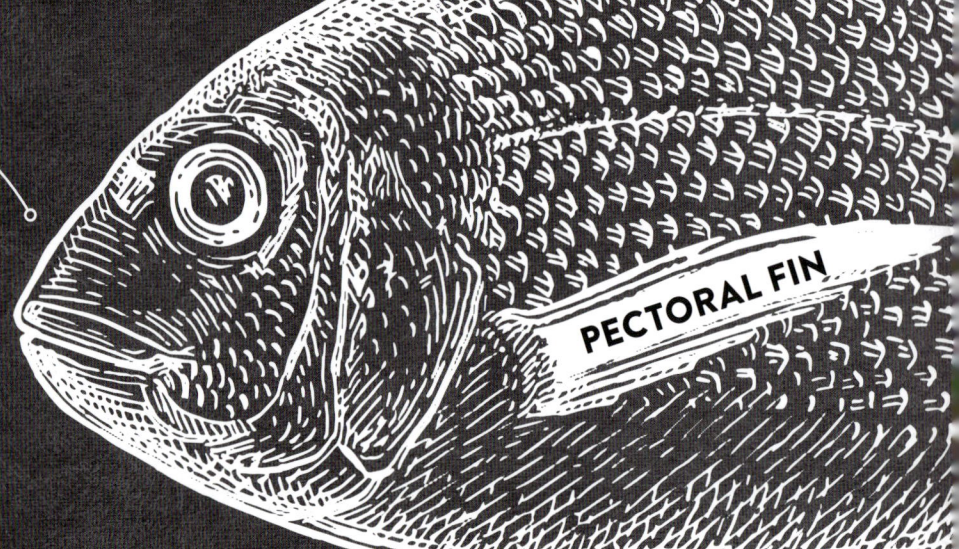

DORSAL FIN

PECTORAL FIN

VENTRAL FIN

Scorpionfish

ARE THERE POISONOUS FISH?

Yes! The most famous are the fish that belong to the order **Scorpionidae**, such as the scorpionfish or the lionfish. These fish have very long **spines** with poisonous glands and colours that allow them to blend in with the seabed, where they lie in wait for their prey.

According to scientific estimates, it seems that about one million species of animals live in the oceans, although it is impossible to know the exact number. Imagine, scientists believe 91% of ocean species are still yet to be classified! The most 'famous' inhabitants of seas and oceans are fish, varied in shapes, sizes and colours.

SCALES

Fish scales are made of keratin. They can be tiny, making the fish seem 'naked', or very large, creating a sort of armour.

CAUDAL FIN

In coordination with the other fins, the caudal fin, or back fin, is a locomotion organ that pushing the fish through the water. It is made of bony spines and webbed skin.

COLOURS

Fish are really colourful! Some are bright in colour, others are covered in stripes or polka dots. Through their numerous colours, many species are able to camouflage themselves to avoid predators and also to recognize other members of their species.

ANAL FIN

WHAT ARE ARMOURED FISH?

Armoured fish belong to the order **Ostraciidae**, equipped with special 'armoured' scales, which leave only the eyes, tail, mouth and fins uncovered. Some species have spikes on the tail and forehead.

Boxfish

NOT ONLY FISH

Manatee
(sirenian)

WHAT ARE MARINE MAMMALS?

Marine mammals have adapted to living in aquatic environments, but, like land mammals, they must return to the surface to breathe. The main groups of mammals living in seas and oceans are: **cetaceans**, which include whales, dolphins and orcas; **sirenians**, which include manatees and dugongs; and **carnivores**, which include walruses and seals.

Orca
(cetacean)

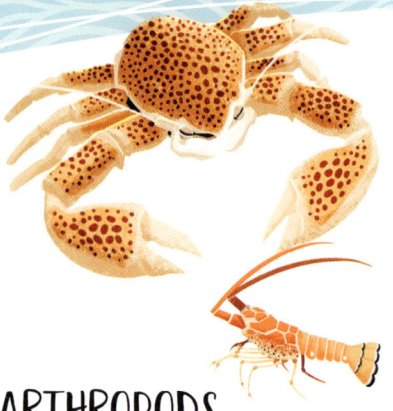

MOLLUSCS

Molluscs have a **soft body**, sometimes with a hard shell. This group includes oysters, which have two shells; snails, which often live attached to other animals; and octopuses, equipped with tentacles.

ARTHROPODS

Arthropods belong to the **crustaceans**. Their body is covered in an **exoskeleton**, a rigid shell that protects them and gives them their shape, which is divided into segments, like legs. Small crustaceans, such as plankton, are essential to the diet of certain cetaceans.

PORIFERA

More commonly known as '**sponges**', these multicellular aquatic animals move imperceptibly. Most belong to the class of demosponge, which are made of soft, elastic fibres. There are also classes of calcareous and of siliceous sponges.

*Not only fish live in the seas and oceans,
but also numerous species of marine mammals, reptiles (especially turtles),
birds and invertebrates, which make up about 95% of marine fauna.*

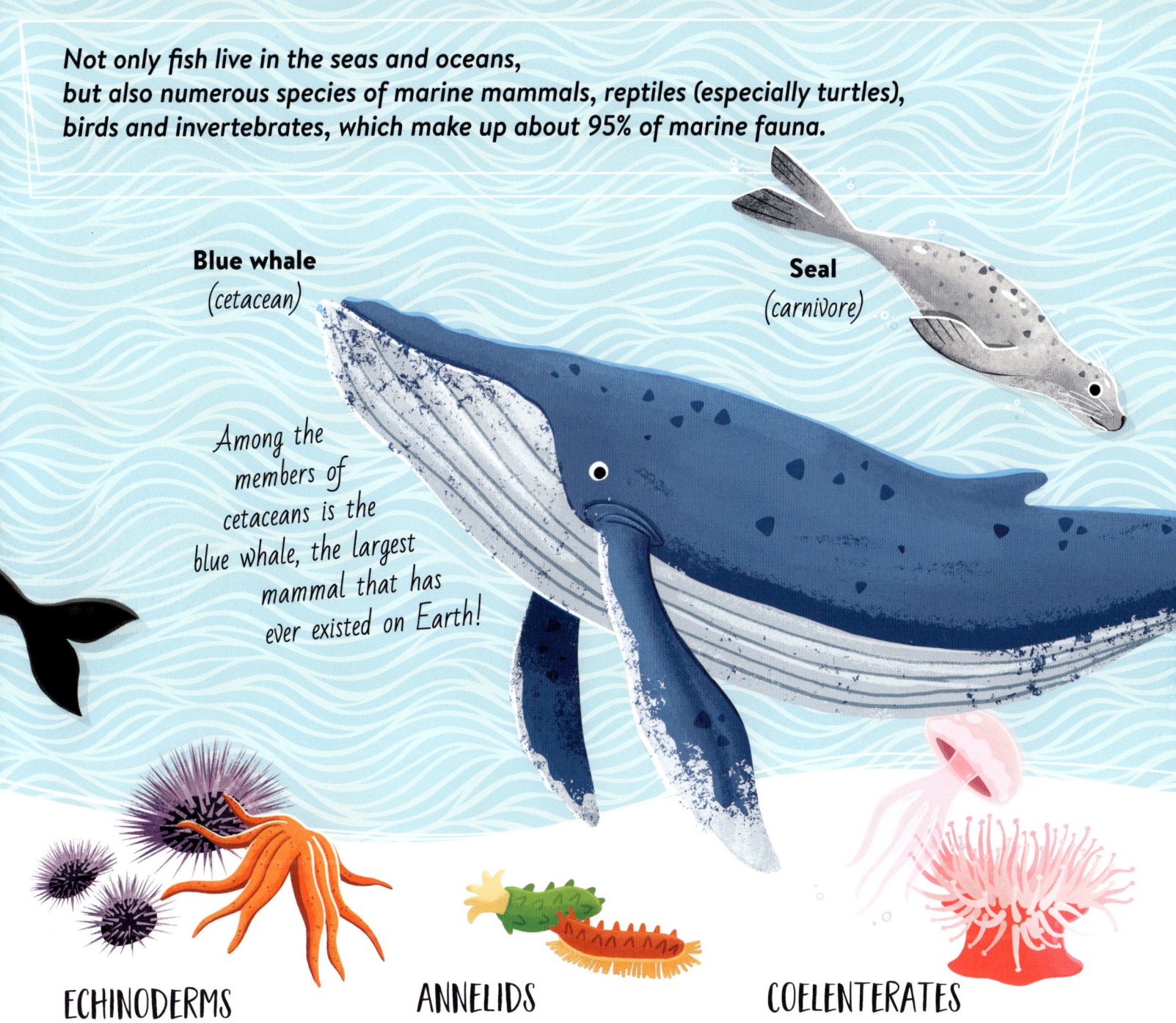

Blue whale
(cetacean)

Seal
(carnivore)

Among the members of cetaceans is the blue whale, the largest mammal that has ever existed on Earth!

ECHINODERMS

This group includes, among others, **starfish**, **sea lilies** and **sea urchins**. Most are small, although some specimens, such as certain starfish, can reach lengths of several metres/feet. They have a **limestone skeleton** and many colours.

ANNELIDS

These are **marine worms**, with an elongated body divided into segments, equipped with parapodia and bristles, for moving around. They are divided into **wandering polychaetes**, which travel on the seafloor, and **sedentary polychaetes**, which live in tubes anchored to the seafloor or in tunnels dug into the sand.

COELENTERATES

These can take one of two forms: the **octopus** or the **jellyfish**.
Both have a central mouth surrounded by tentacles, but octopuses live anchored to the seafloor with their tentacles facing up, whereas jellyfish direct their tentacles facing down and have an umbrella-like shape.

41

ARE THERE MANY SPECIES OF MARINE REPTILES?

In fact, once upon a time, during the **Age of the Dinosaurs**, there were many more marine reptiles. Today, however, there are fewer: These species are found in sea turtles, marine iguanas, saltwater crocodiles and sea snakes.

The marine iguana can tolerate very cold temperatures and excrete large amounts of salt.

Belcher's sea snake is the most venomous snake species in the world!

The saltwater crocodile is the largest reptile on Earth!

WHAT ARE THE OLDEST MARINE REPTILES?

Turtles! They are not only the oldest marine reptiles but also the longest-surviving members of the entire order of reptiles. And throughout their existence on Earth, they have maintained their characteristic features. Until 200 years ago, there were millions of specimens populating the seas and oceans. Today, however, their numbers have fallen dramatically and many species are considered **endangered**.

The leatherback sea turtle is the largest turtle on the planet. Imagine, it can weigh up to an average of 450 kilograms (992 pounds)! It travels thousands of kilometres, and the female turtles return to the beach where they were born to lay their eggs.

1.8–2.2 m (6–7.2 ft)

250–700 kg (550–1,540 lbs)

DO BIRDS ALSO LIVE IN THE SEAS AND OCEANS?

Birds do not really live in water, but there are various species that have adapted to live in **very close contact with the sea**. Here they find food to nourish themselves, such as fish, plankton and crustaceans. Several species nest on the cliffs or along the coasts, but all share particular traits: **webbed feet**, **waterproof feathers**, **tapered bodies** suitable for both swimming and flying...and little ability to walk on land.

WHAT IS THE LARGEST SEABIRD?

The largest seabird is the **albatross**, which has the widest wingspan on Earth. This bird can fly for days and days without stopping. It does stop to nest or to reproduce. When there is a good wind, the albatross can stay aloft for many hours without having to flap its wings, which are long and narrow. Like other sea birds, the albatross also drinks sea water; it feeds mainly on squid, but at times may also approach ships to feed on refuse.

12 kg
(26.5 lbs)

2–3.4 m (6.6–11 ft)

DO ALL SEABIRDS FLY?

No, not all of them, for example: **penguins**. Thanks to their hydrodynamic shape, penguins, rather, are very skilled swimmers, who can dive many metres deep and hold their breath for several minutes to chase prey. On land they move in a very particular way, and their slow pace allows them to save a lot of energy.

Emperor penguin

43

AN ECOSYSTEM AT RISK

POLLUTION

Factories and industrial plants often dump their **waste** into the waters of the seas and oceans. Add to this waste an incredible amount of **plastic and microplastic**, which is swallowed by the seas' and oceans' inhabitants, becoming part of the food chain—ours too! To make matters worse, humans are responsible for the **petroleum entering the water**, in different quantities, from ships crossing the seas and oceans.

GLOBAL WARMING

Global warming causes **sea levels to rise**, alters the **chemistry** of the oceans, interferes with many of the processes taking place there and threatens many different animal species, unable to survive the **ever-increasing temperatures**. Furthermore, **greenhouse gases** cause climate change making the sea and ocean water absorb much more carbon dioxide, turning it acidic, which threatens corals and many types of plankton, the basis of the marine food chain.

AIR POLLUTION

Air pollution is responsible for nearly one-third of the **toxic substances** that end up in coastal areas and oceans. These pollutants, such as sulphur dioxide and mercury produced by coal-fired power plants, are carried by the air.

The ecosystem of the seas and oceans is at risk, above all due to human activities, activities directly in the aquatic environment or along the coasts and also activities inland. Imagine, more than 80% of marine pollution comes from land-based activities! Let's have a look at some of the most serious threats to the ecosystem!

OVERFISHING

The number of fish that are caught is unsustainable, in which dangerous and harmful techniques are used damaging the marine ecosystem, such as **trawling**: giant nets are dragged on the seabed, collecting and crushing anything. This type of high-impact fishing destroys already very fragile habitats, such coral reefs, as well as other creatures, such as fish, turtles and manta rays, which become entangled in the nets. Many of these species are already in danger of extinction.

INVASIVE SPECIES

Due to both human activity and climate change, many **invasive species**, such as poisonous algae, marine plants or animals, migrate to new places. This upsets the ecological balance of the seas and oceans, because non-endemic species 'invade', disrupting the fragile balance of the ecosystem. One example is **killer algae**, one of the hundred most harmful invasive alien species in the world, which proliferate without any natural enemy to stop them in a new environment, producing **harmful substances** for the local marine herbivores.

PESTICIDES AND FERTILIZERS

Pesticides and **fertilizers** used in agriculture reach the sea, depleting the water of the oxygen necessary for the life of molluscs and marine plants: creating vast dead zones, in which many species struggle to survive.

CREATURES IN DANGER

Because of the threats to the marine ecosystem, many animal species are at risk of extinction. Let's have a look at some of them. The category of threat will be indicated for each as identified by the IUCN (International Union for the Conservation of Nature).

ENDANGERED

The **vaquita** is easily recognized by the dark rings around the eyes. It is a marine mammal in serious danger of extinction. In recent years, their numbers have severely dropped, especially because they are often captured and drowned by the nets used during illegal fishing in the marine protected areas in the Gulf of California.

The enormous **Napoleonfish** lives in the coral reef and can measure more than 2 metres (6 feet) in length. Its survival is threatened by the live coral reef fish trade, mainly in Southeast Asia. Poachers, in fact, use highly destructive and illegal fishing methods to catch these fish.

CRITICALLY ENDANGERED

The **loggerhead turtle** is the most common turtle in the Mediterranean. It breeds on the coasts of Greece and Turkey, and is very important because it helps maintain the health of coral reefs. Its survival is threatened both by accidental capture in fishing equipment and by tourism development on the beaches where it nests.

VULNERABLE

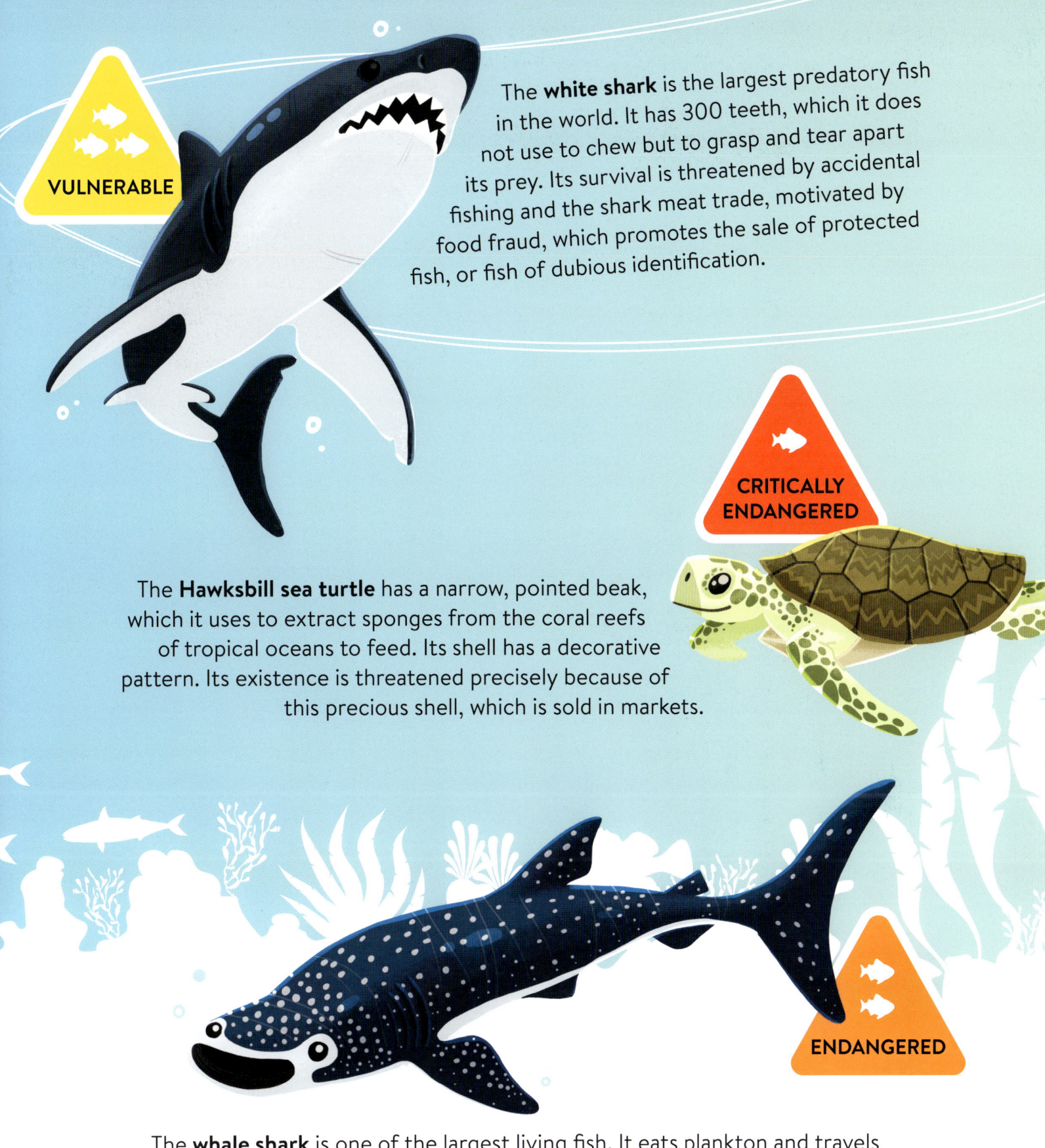

The **white shark** is the largest predatory fish in the world. It has 300 teeth, which it does not use to chew but to grasp and tear apart its prey. Its survival is threatened by accidental fishing and the shark meat trade, motivated by food fraud, which promotes the sale of protected fish, or fish of dubious identification.

The **Hawksbill sea turtle** has a narrow, pointed beak, which it uses to extract sponges from the coral reefs of tropical oceans to feed. Its shell has a decorative pattern. Its existence is threatened precisely because of this precious shell, which is sold in markets.

The **whale shark** is one of the largest living fish. It eats plankton and travels great distances to find enough to support its large size. Its body is covered in white spots, which make it easily recognizable. Today these sharks are protected in many countries, but unfortunately, in some oceans of the world their populations are falling dramatically due to illegal fishing.

WHAT SOLUTIONS ARE THERE?

Much has been done and much is being done by international groups to safeguard the marine ecosystem. It is very important that each of us, in our own small way, adopts behaviours that are respectful of the planet, for example by collecting plastic waste on the beaches or by limiting activities that pollute the environment! Below we will look at some of the most useful solutions that have been adopted to safeguard the seas and oceans.

WHAT ARE MARINE PROTECTED AREAS?

Marine protected areas are where governments have decided to place **limits on human activity**. In these areas, for example, it is not possible to fish, extract materials or destroy natural resources. There are many reasons these reserves are established. They are created to **protect marine species** in danger of extinction, and are also used as **laboratories**: in this way, researchers can compare the areas affected by human activities with those where human activity has been reduced to a minimum.

Ang Thong National Marine Park, Thailand

The Pelagos Sanctuary was established in the Tyrrhenian Sea in 1999, covering 96,000 km² (37,065 mi²) of sea surface. During the summer months, many species of cetaceans that live in the Mediterranean Sea gather here, because this area is rich in plankton. Here, these marine mammals are protected by strict regulation, which prevents them from being disturbed. For example, it is required to moderate the boat speed and maintain a distance from these creatures.

HOW ARE CORAL REEFS BEING PROTECTED?

Coral reefs are one of the most fragile marine habitats. For this reason they require even greater attention! Some of the solutions to protect them include:

the creation in the laboratory of **artificial coral reefs** with special materials, to recreate a habitat suitable for the inhabitants of the coral reefs that are disappearing;

the development in the laboratory of **special plants** able to feed the weakened corals in an artificial way;

and the **protection of the less vulnerable barriers** from climate change and pollution, to make them a suitable refuge for the inhabitants of the weakest reefs.

HOW ARE OIL SPILLS CONTAINED?

To contain oil spills in the seas and oceans, **floating containment barriers** are often used, which are placed around the affected area to limit the spread of oil and to channel it into man-made pools, where it is easier to remove from the surface. **Skimmers** (or separators) are also used, which are automatic or operated by a ship. These separate the oil from the water. In the case of more limited spills, **absorbents** are used: special materials that absorb and retain the pollutant.

THE SEA AND EXPLORATION

3500 BCE–500 BCE

790 CE–1066 CE

WHO WERE THE FIRST GREAT NAVIGATORS?

The **Phoenicians**. They used their strategic location, present-day Lebanon, to build a vast trading empire. The most famous Phoenician maritime expedition was the 'Periplus of Hanno' which took place between the 7th and 5th centuries BCE. The great navigator Hanno left from Carthage (the most important Phoenician colony), crossed the Pillars of Hercules (the Strait of Gibraltar) and, skirting the African coasts to the south, reached the Gulf of Bonny, Nigeria.

EXPLORERS FROM THE NORTH...

The **Vikings** were fierce warriors and also expert navigators. From the Nordic sagas, we know that they discovered different lands by sea: Greenland in 980 CE by Erik the Red and, unwittingly, America by Leif Erikson (Erik's son), who reached the islands of Baffin and Newfoundland.

Even in the past, centuries ago, the sea was a favourite way to discover the world, unknown lands and distant peoples. Navigation has allowed humanity to encounter new cultures and overseas countries.

WHAT WAS HAPPENING IN THE EAST?

Between 1405 and 1433, the Chinese Empire organized sea expeditions led by **Zheng He**, admiral of the imperial fleet. During the first expedition, the fleet reached as far as Vietnam, Borneo and Malaysia. Then He headed for Java, Sumatra and Indonesia, arriving in Sri Lanka and India. The fifth expedition took the admiral to Africa, to the ports of Aden, Mogadishu and Malindi.

1271 CE–1292 CE

1405 CE–1433 CE

1434 CE

THE SILK ROAD

Marco Polo, a Venetian merchant, wanted to travel the entire Silk Road, the most important trade route between Europe and the East. On his outward journey, he travelled some sections by land and others by sea. On the other hand, his return journey he made entirely by sea. In 1292 he departed once again travelling a route completely by sea, sailing the coasts of Vietnam, Malaysia, Sumatra and India, then arriving in Trebizond and finally in Venice.

DISCOVERING AFRICA IN THE MIDDLE AGES

Africa was still unknown to Europe during the Middle Ages, and what was believed to be known about this continent held little truth. Because of this, even the bravest adventurers dared not travel beyond Cape Bojador on the northern coast of the Sahara. Only in the 15th century did someone dare, even if not in person: In 1432 **Henry the Navigator**, a wealthy Portuguese prince, financed the expedition of his squire Gil Eannes, who travelled passed Cape Bojador.

ROUTE TO AMERICA

In 1492 **Cristoforo Colombo** wanted to find a route to the East without circumnavigating Africa. He left from Palos in Spain with two caravels, the *Niña* and the *Pinta*, and a carrack, the *Santa Maria*. He stopped over in the Canaries, then crossed the Sargasso Sea, until he reached an island in the Bahamas. The fleet wandered between the Caribbean islands and, on seeing Cuba, Columbus thought he had reached what is today Japan. He sailed the north coast of Haiti, and, with some difficulties, returned to Portugal. Without knowing, Columbus had opened a route between Europe and America.

1487 CE

1492 CE

1497 CE

A NEW ROUTE TO THE EAST?

In 1487 **Bartolomeo Diaz** was given command of the fleet formed by the king of Portugal, John II, with the aim of finding a new route to the Indian Ocean. Arriving in the southernmost part of Africa, Diaz's fleet was surprised by a violent storm, which carried the ships as far as the Indian Ocean. On the way back, Diaz mapped the coasts he had not been able to observe on the way out due to the storm. The southernmost Cape of Africa was named the Cape of Good Hope.

WHO WAS VASCO DA GAMA?

Vasco da Gama, for his explorations, relied on Bartolomeo Diaz's notes and maps. He was a young Portuguese navigator who, in 1497, was entrusted with an expedition to open a new route to the Indies, circumnavigating Africa. He crossed the Cape of Good Hope, stopped over in Mozambique and Mombasa, reaching as far as Malindi. From there, he crossed the Atlantic Ocean and reached Calicut, India.

WHEN DID WE CIRCUMNAVIGATE THE EARTH FOR THE FIRST TIME?

In 1519. The idea came to a Portuguese navigator, **Ferdinand Magellan**, who was convinced that in South America there was a passage to reach Asia. After an exhausting voyage, Magellan and his fleet arrived in South America, spent the winter in the Gulf of San Julián and, after months of sailing, landed in the Philippine Islands. They arrived at their destination in 1521, the Maluku Islands in the Indian Ocean, and then returned to Spain in 1522. With his journey, Magellan proved definitively that the earth is spherical and that all oceans connect with each other.

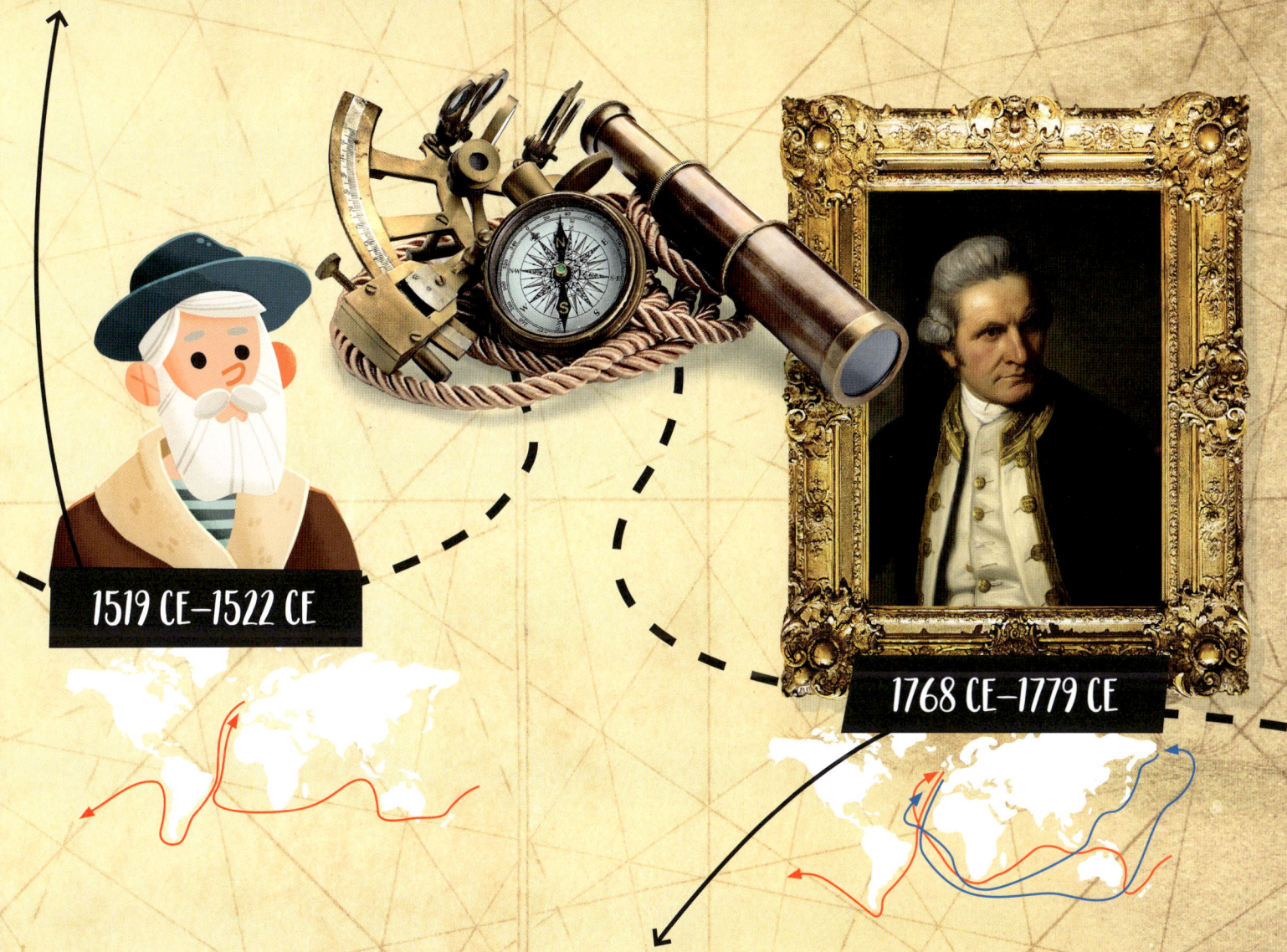

1519 CE–1522 CE

1768 CE–1779 CE

WHO EXPLORED THE ISLANDS OF THE PACIFIC?

James Cook. He was commissioned by the British Royal Society to set out on an exploratory voyage of the Pacific Ocean. He left in 1768 and in three years made detailed surveys around New Zealand and along the eastern coasts of Australia. He reached Antarctica in 1772 and then set out in search of the Northwest Passage, a trade route westward from the Atlantic to the Pacific ocean. He then headed for the west coast of North America trying in vain to explore the coasts of Siberia and Alaska to find a passage to the Atlantic. He failed and was forced to return to Hawaii, where he was killed.

EXPLORATION TODAY

Today the discovery of new and unknown lands on Earth has almost reached its end. Instead, we seek to discover what is hidden beneath the surface of the seas and oceans: the ocean depths, the ocean floor, is an underwater world still largely unknown.

WHY WE EXPLORE THE OCEANS?

Exploring the oceans allows us to understand them better in order to **protect** them, as well as to **use their resources** in the most effective and least harmful way possible. This is why chemical, physical, geological and biological aspects of the oceans are documented. Studies do not concern only the saltwater expanses but also many other aspects that closely affect life on land. Studies of the oceans and their ecosystems, in fact:

offer new information for technology and engineering innovations;

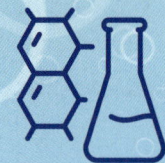

are useful in finding, for example, new sources for sustainable medicine, food and energy;

help us understand how to respond to dangers such as earthquakes and tsunamis;

help us understand our effect on the oceans and how we are effected by the changes on Earth.

If we removed all the water that covers the earth, we would observe a familiar landscape: plains, deep valleys and mountains. Imagine, some of the sea mountains are so high that we can see them on land!

The tallest mountain on Earth, in fact, is Mount Pico, in the Azores: it measures 2,351 metres (7,713 feet) above sea level, but the water hides another 6,098 metres (20,006 feet)!

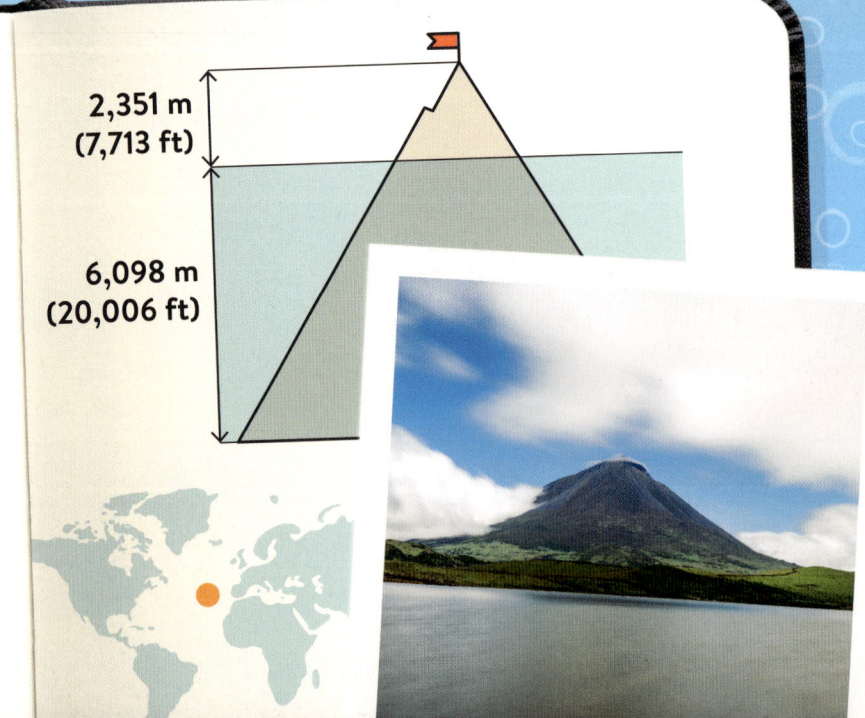

2,351 m (7,713 ft)

6,098 m (20,006 ft)

HOW IS UNDERWATER EXPLORATION POSSIBLE?

There are two types of **underwater exploration: direct** or **indirect**. The first is accomplished by human beings who deep-sea dive, using, for example, submerged bathyscaphes and laboratories. This type of exploration, however, is risky and requires years of training. Indirect measurements of the oceans can also be accomplished using **sonar** or **echo sounding**, which measure the distance between the surface and the seafloor through sound pulses. Today, **drones** and **robots** equipped with surface-controlled cameras are being sent to the bottom of the sea.

WHY DOES NASA STUDY THE OCEAN DEPTHS?

To **experiment with techniques and equipment** that will be used during space missions. Often, in fact, before departures astronauts are sent on underwater missions. In addition, studying the oceans is a way to understand the functioning of the water expanses and the presence of life on other planets.

Finally, questions that directly concern Earth are studied. For example, hydrothermal springs have been reproduced to understand **how life originated on Earth.** During some space missions, important surveys have been made from Space on climate, ocean circulation and 'water' salinity.

NASA's ocean explorations have led to knowledge and technologies that are used today in **oceanographic research:** for measuring the topography of the ocean floor, the oceanic winds and the ocean's colour.

THE SEA IN MYTHS AND LEGENDS

Over the centuries, the mystery that surrounds the sea and everything beneath its surface has led to tales and legends of mythical and mysterious creatures that dwell in the underwater world, stories passed down and shared, even today offering ideas for movies or books. Let's read about some of them!

GODS OF THE SEA

According to Roman mythology, **Neptune** was the god of the sea, considered the protector of those who sail. In Greek mythology, this god corresponds to **Poseidon**, one of the many sons of Zeus, who, in addition to being the god of the sea, is the god of tsunamis, earthquakes and of all the underwater kingdom. He is often portrayed as a vengeful and cantankerous god, capable of giving life to monstrous creatures and unleashing the most dangerous natural forces.

In Greek mythology, there is also a goddess of the sea, Tethys, wife of the titan Oceanus, with whom she had more than 3,000 children, which correspond to all the waters of the world.

ATLANTIS

It was the philosopher **Plato** who first wrote of the city of Atlantis. In his story, Atlantis is an ancient civilization, whose founders were half-god and half-human. The inhabitants of Atlantis were very rich and lived in magnificent houses and had temples filled with gold, silver and other precious metals. According to the Greek philosopher, the people of Atlantis, however, became so greedy and dishonest that the gods decided to punish them, so they **made the island disappear**. It is said that this island is located somewhere in the Atlantic Ocean.

THE KRAKEN

One of the most famous mythological sea creatures is the Kraken, a **giant squid** that terrified sailors and passing ships. According to legend, the Kraken lives off the coasts of Greenland and Norway, and it wraps its long tentacles around ships, dragging them to the bottom of the sea. It is thought that the legend comes from the real sightings by some sailors during their voyages of a giant squid of truly remarkable dimensions.

THE FLYING DUTCHMAN

One of the most famous European legends is certainly the Flying Dutchman. This **ghost ship** takes its name from its captain, the Flying Dutchman, condemned to sail the seas for eternity. The ship can make port only once every seven years, so the captain can go to land to seek true love, his only hope of salvation. Sailors believe that if they spot the Flying Dutchman while at sea, it is a harbinger of impending disaster.

SIRENS

Although we imagine mermaids with a body that is half-fish and half-woman, in Greek mythology the sirens were represented as half-bird and half-woman. According to myth, the three original sirens are **Peisinoe**, **Aglaope** and **Thelxiepeia**, who could sing such enchanting melodies to bewitch sailors from their work, and even cause them to wreck their ship against the rocks. One of the most famous stories in which they appear is the *Odyssey*, where the sirens bewitch the protagonist, Odysseus.

LET'S EXPERIMENT!

For all activities ask an adult for help!

OCEAN IN A JAR

We have read that the ocean is divided into different zones. Let's re-create these in a jar!

You will need:

A clear container

A funnel

Food colouring (black and blue) *

An eyedropper

Labels and a marker

1 150 ml (5 oz) of corn syrup

2 150 ml (5 oz) of transparent dish soap

3 150 ml (5 oz) of water

4 150 ml (5 oz) of oil

5 150 ml (5 oz) of colourless denatured alcohol

* To colour the oil, use an oil-based colourant (blue).

1. Begin by preparing the darkest and deepest layer of the ocean (the hadopelagic zone): add and mix a little black food colouring to the corn syrup and pour it into the jar using the funnel.

2. Prepare the layer that corresponds to the abyssopelagic zone: add a little blue dye to the dish soap and pour it into the jar.

3. Prepare the layer that corresponds to the bathypelagic zone: add a few drops of blue food colouring to the water, so that it is a little lighter than the preceding zone, and pour it very slowly over the soap layer using the funnel.

4. Prepare the layer that corresponds to the mesopelagic zone: add a few drops of oil-based blue colouring to the oil. (Make sure it is lighter than the previous layer!) Pour it over the layer of water.

5. Finally, prepare the layer that corresponds to the epipelagic zone: using the dropper, add a drop of blue colouring to the denatured alcohol and pour it over the oil layer, making sure the alcohol does not separate the water and oil.

6. Here is your ocean in a jar! If you want, you can add a small label with the name of the zone written on it to identify the different layers more easily.

1
2
3
4
5
6
Epipelagic zone
Mesopelagic zone
Bathypelagic zone
Abyssopelagic zone
Hadopelagic zone

WARM CURRENTS

In the previous pages we read about the currents. With this simple experiment you will better understand how warm currents behave when they come into contact with cold water.

You will need:

A clear or white tray

Cold water

Food colouring (blue and red)

Ice cubes

Boiling water

1 Pour half a litre/quart of cold water into the tray and add a few drops of blue food colouring—not too many, however, or you may not see the currents!

2 Add the ice cubes and let them melt. The goal is to make the water as cold as possible. While the ice melts, boil half a litre/quart of water. Once the water is boiling, add a few drops of red food colouring, then gradually pour it into a corner of the tray containing the cold water.

3 See how currents are formed! The hot water pushes through the cold water and moves quickly forming strips. In addition, notice the eddies that form, that is, the circular currents in motion.

WATER ACIDIFICATION

One of the most serious threats to the marine ecosystem is water acidification. In this experiment, you will discover how acidity affects some organisms.

You will need:

Glasses   Shells   Salt water *   Labels and a marker   White vinegar

* To make salt water, add 1 teaspoon of salt to 1 glass of water.

1 Place a shell in each glass. Fill a glass with salt water and put a label on it to identify it: write on the label 'salt water'. Fill all the other glasses with vinegar, completely covering the shells. This way you can compare the reactions.

Salt water

2 After having poured the vinegar on the shells, you will notice that as time passes, more bubbles of carbon dioxide form, the shells become fragile, and they eventually break into pieces because of the chemical reaction.

This is what happens in the sea when the water becomes too acidic!

OIL SPILL

In the previous pages, we read that one of the causes of the pollution of the seas and oceans is oil spills. With this experiment, you will better understand what happens when oil spreads in the waves.

You will need:

A clear, deep container

Water

Blue food colouring

A spoon

Small stones

Plastic fish

A plastic boat

A glass

Oil

Cocoa powder

Cotton balls and a sponge

1. Fill the container halfway with water and add 1-2 drops of the blue food colouring. Stir with the spoon.

2. Re-create the ocean habitat using small stones and plastic fish. Once you're done, place the plastic boat on the surface.

3. Now colour the oil to make it look more like petroleum: in a glass mix the oil and cocoa powder.

4. Pour the oil into the boat, as if it were a tanker transporting oil across the ocean, then turn the boat over to simulate an 'oil spill' in the ocean. This is what happens when ships have accidents!

5. Try removing the oil from the water with a spoon, a cotton ball and a sponge. You will find how difficult it is to remove the oil from the water: the more you try, the more it seems to spread!

© 2022 Sassi Editore Srl
Viale Roma 122/b
36015 Schio (VI) - Italy

Text: Giulia Pesavento
Illustrations: Enrico Lorenzi
Design: Alberto Borgo
Translation: SallyAnn DelVino

This Walker book belongs to

To Eva, Florence and Kit, who are just beginning their journey through history – P.P.

For Shaun, for looking after everything so I have the time to draw.
And for Mum and Dad, all those museum trips finally came in handy – L.K.

First published 2021 by Walker Books Ltd, 87 Vauxhall Walk, London SE11 5HJ 2 4 6 8 10 9 7 5 3 1 Text © 2021 Philip Parker Illustrations © 2021 Liz Kay The right of Philip Parker and Liz Kay to be identified as author and illustrator respectively of this work has been asserted by them in accordance with the Copyright, Designs and Patents Act 1988 This book has been typeset in Agenda Printed in Thailand All rights reserved. No part of this book may be reproduced, transmitted or stored in an information retrieval system in any form or by any means, graphic, electronic or mechanical, including photocopying, taping and recording, without prior written permission from the publisher. British Library Cataloguing in Publication Data: a catalogue record for this book is available from the British Library ISBN 978-1-4063-9121-3 www.walker.co.uk

WALKER BOOKS
AND SUBSIDIARIES
LONDON · BOSTON · SYDNEY · AUCKLAND

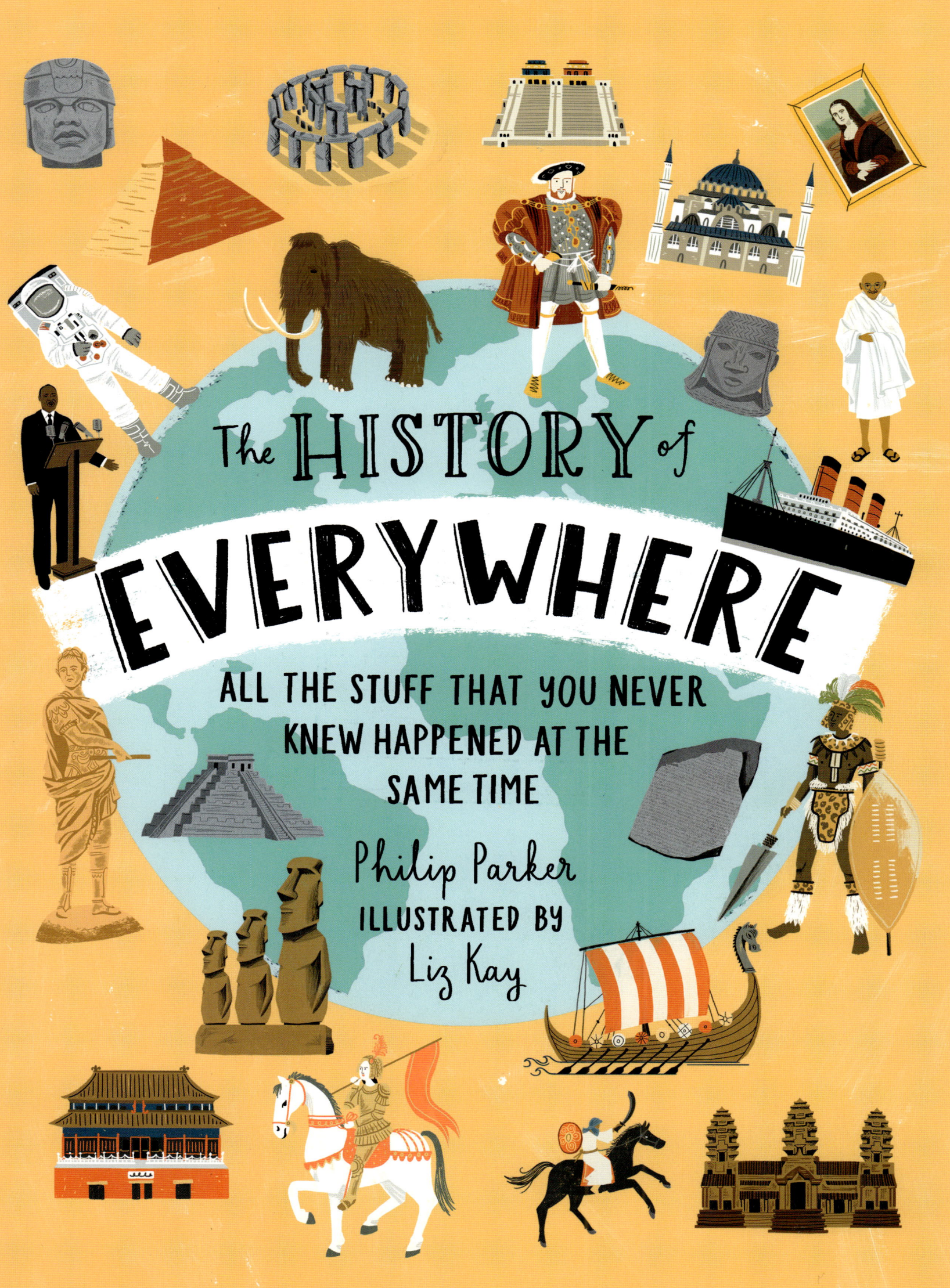

The HISTORY of EVERYWHERE

ALL THE STUFF THAT YOU NEVER KNEW HAPPENED AT THE SAME TIME

Philip Parker

ILLUSTRATED BY
Liz Kay

INTRODUCTION

HISTORY CAN SEEM a confusing and complex subject. Civilisations rise and fall, and the connections between them can be hard to understand. Everywhere has its own story to tell – and it's only if we look at the whole world of history that we can appreciate its richness and wonder.

In this book you'll find maps showing what was happening all over the world in any one period. You can see that China and Rome had emperors at the same time, that there were still woolly mammoths roaming around while the Egyptians were building their pyramids, and much more.

We can't cover everything, otherwise the book would weigh as much as a mammoth, but hope it will inspire you to explore some more of history's amazing tales. To get you started, each era has one fascinating key event picked out in more detail. Some civilisations, such as the ancient Greeks, Egyptians or the Mughals of India, also have their own pages about their special contributions to the world and how they fit into the jigsaw puzzle of history.

History hasn't stopped. The events we are living through today will appear in next year's history books. History is always weaving new stories and new connections: we sometimes just need a little help to see them.

CONTENTS

4000-1000 BC THE FIRST CIVILISATIONS

The earliest civilisations were based around cities with huge monumental buildings. These civilisations began to struggle with their neighbours for control of resources like iron and gold, leading to the first wars. Among them, the Egyptians and Hittites were two kingdoms who fought for power in the Mediterranean.

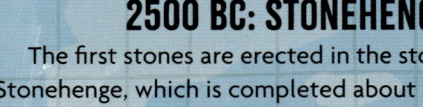

2500 BC: STONEHENGE

The first stones are erected in the stone circle at Stonehenge, which is completed about 300 years later.

NORTH AMERICA

EUROPE

4000 BC: GROWING CROPS

Farming begins in North America as people learn to grow maize, beans and squash. The first ever farmers lived in what is now Iraq, around 10,000 BC.

2550 BC: PYRAMIDS

The Egyptian pharaoh Khufu orders the construction of the Great Pyramid of Giza. Originally about 150 metres high and built with 2.3 million stone blocks, it serves as Khufu's burial place and is one of over 130 royal pyramids built over the next 700 years.

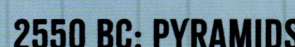

1200 BC: OLMECS

The Olmec culture, the oldest in Central America, develops. Its people carve monumental stone sculptures, including 3.5-metre high heads.

SOUTH AMERICA

C. 1000 BC: BANTU MIGRATION

Bantu-speaking people begin to migrate from West Africa into central Africa. They bring with them knowledge of farming and reach modern South Africa by about AD 500.

2800 BC: CITY OF CARAL

The Norte Chico people of the Pacific coast establish Caral, the first city in the Americas, building temples, pyramids and plazas.

KEY EVENT: BATTLE OF KADESH

The oldest battle of which we have a proper description was in May 1274 BC, when the Egyptian pharaoh Ramesses II led his army into Palestine to prevent the Hittite people conquering it. He ran into a Hittite force near Kadesh and a massive chariot fight took place. It was so hard-fought that both sides claimed victory.

DID YOU KNOW?

The world's earliest writing systems developed in ancient Egypt and Sumer (in modern Iraq). The Egyptians used picture-like symbols to represent words, while the Sumerian script is written using wedge shapes that make up syllables.

GREECE

1600 BC: MYCENAEANS

The Mycenaeans, a warrior people, build palaces throughout southern Greece. They conquer the Minoans, Europe's earliest civilisation, on Crete.

2500 BC: INDUS VALLEY

Mohenjo-Daro is one of the largest towns of the Indus Valley civilisation in South Asia, with public baths and the world's first sewage system. The Indus Valley script, which appears on thousands of clay seals, has not been deciphered.

C. 2000 BC: WOOLLY MAMMOTHS

The last woolly mammoths, who had survived on islands off the coast of Alaska, finally become extinct.

1600 BC: SHANG DYNASTY

The Shang, China's first recorded dynasty, rules over part of the north of the country. Its craftsmen make elaborate bronze vessels for ceremonial use.

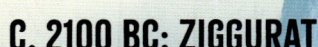

C. 2100 BC: ZIGGURAT

In the Sumerian city of Ur, a great stepped temple-pyramid, called a ziggurat, is built with mud-bricks. It is over 30 metres high.

1500 BC: LAPITA PEOPLE

The Lapita people, known for their decorated pottery, begin to migrate from South East Asia into the Pacific islands.

C. 50,000 BC: ABORIGINES

Aboriginal people first arrive in Australia over 50,000 years ago. They spread across the continent, recording their beliefs about mythical ancestors in paintings in caves and on rocks.

AFRICA

N
W   E
S

1000–500 BC THE FIRST EMPIRES

As city states became richer and more powerful, rulers emerged who conquered their neighbours to create the first empires. Assyrian armies captured much of the Middle East, while in China the Zhou Dynasty struggled to control its many states. This was a time of great cultural and religious change: in Greece the first scientists and philosophers composed their works, and in India the Buddhist religion developed.

776 BC: OLYMPICS

The first recorded Olympic Games are held at Olympia in Greece. At first there are just foot races, but later boxing, wrestling, chariot races and the discus are added. Victors win laurel wreaths.

1000 BC: ADENA PEOPLE

The Adena culture in the eastern woodlands of North America build large earth burial mounds, some in the shape of animals such as snakes.

NORTH AMERICA

753 BC: ROME

The city of Rome is founded in Italy, according to legend by the brothers Romulus and Remus.

ROME

732 BC: NUBIANS

The Nubian ruler Piye conquers Egypt, beginning a period when it is mainly controlled by foreign rulers.

C. 900 BC: OLMEC ART

The Olmecs build an adobe (clay) pyramid, and produce mosaic floors representing jaguars and mirrors made of iron.

CAMEROON

900 BC: CHAVÍN PEOPLE

The Chavín people in northern Peru build a massive temple complex at Chavín de Huantar, filled with fantastic carvings of feline and snake-like figures.

SOUTH AMERICA

C. 500 BC: HANNO THE NAVIGATOR

The Phoenician explorer Hanno the Navigator sails from Carthage, in the Mediterranean, to the west coast of Africa. He founds several cities in modern Morocco and may have reached as far as Cameroon.

N
W E
S

KEY EVENT: THE BIRTH OF BUDDHA

In 534 BC, Siddhartha Gautama, a prince of the Sakya people in India, renounced his privileged life and became a monk to try to find a way to understand human suffering. Finally, while meditating under a pipal tree, he achieved a state of enlightenment, realising he could escape the endless cycle of rebirth and suffering. He taught people to reject attachment to earthly desires and his followers wrote down his sermons, which became the basis of the Buddhist religion. This spread from India into China, Korea, Japan and South East Asia.

587 BC: JERUSALEM DESTRUCTION

The Babylonian king Nebuchadnezzar II orders the destruction of Jerusalem and its Temple after a Jewish revolt. Most Jewish people go into exile.

GREECE

EGYPT

660 BC: JAPAN'S FIRST EMPEROR

Jimmu Tenno, the first emperor of Japan, ascends to the throne. He is the ancestor of today's Japanese ruling house, making it the longest-lasting dynasty in history.

JAPAN

551 BC: CONFUCIUS

The philosopher Confucius is born. His ideas about the importance of traditional rituals, respecting hierarchy and knowledge as the basis of a good life and society are influential in China for over 2,000 years.

CHINA

INDIA

VIETNAM

1000 BC: VIETNAM BRONZE

Craftsmen from the Dong Son culture in northern Vietnam make huge, elaborately decorated bronze drums to use during rituals and military campaigns.

590 BC: PYRAMIDS

Meroë becomes the capital of the kingdom of Kush in modern Sudan. Its rulers build more pyramids than the Egyptians, though they are smaller.

C. 500 BC: LONGEST POEM

The Mahabharata, the longest-ever epic poem at 100,000 verses, is composed. It tells of the Kurukshetra War, including battles on war elephants, and may reflect the political situation in Iron Age India.

DID YOU KNOW?

The Hanging Gardens of Babylon, one of the Seven Wonders of the Ancient World, are believed to have been in the magnificent city rebuilt by Nebuchadnezzar II between 605 and 562 BC. Babylon was conquered by the Persians in 539 BC.

FOCUS ON
ANCIENT GREECE
DEMOCRACY AND PHILOSOPHY

Ancient Greece was made up of a large number of cities (known as city states), which ruled a small area around them. Some, such as Sparta, were ruled by kings. Others, like Sparta's main rival Athens, replaced the kings and oligarchs (small groups of families) with a different form of government. In this early form of democracy (government by the people), people gathered together to vote on important decisions. In city states which were democracies the atmosphere was freer than those where kings ruled, and some people, called philosophers, rejected the traditional idea that the gods controlled the world. Instead, they began to think of alternative explanations for how it had come to be the way that it was. Ancient Greek democracy and philosophy would influence the world for hundreds of years.

ATHENS

THE ASSEMBLY

BUILDING A DEMOCRACY

Athens was at first ruled by oligarchs and tyrants (men with the power of a king, but who were not from a royal family). In 507 BC a man called Kleisthenes abolished the old system and introduced the world's first democracy. From then on 500 Athenian citizens were chosen each year at random, who could decide which laws to pass. Then, an assembly of all citizens who wished to attend gathered, and voted whether to accept those laws. Unlike our modern democracy, where politicians are elected to pass laws, in the Athenian, direct democracy, citizens had to attend the assembly in person to vote. Juries for trials and some officials who ran the city's services were also chosen at random. As well as passing laws, the assembly made decisions on whether to declare war, and elected the generals to lead the Athenian army.

PHILOSOPHY

Around 600 BC, Greek philosophers began to think that it was not the gods, but natural forces which shaped the world. They tried to work out what substance made up the world, and also developed theories about the best way to live our lives and the best manner in which to organise society. These are some of the most famous thinkers in ancient Greece.

LIVING IN A DEMOCRACY

Athenian democracy was not open to everyone and only free adult male citizens could attend the assembly and vote. Women, slaves and foreigners were not allowed to do so. To prevent any politicians from becoming too powerful in the assembly, once each year Athenians were allowed to carry out a special vote called an ostracism. They scratched the name of a politician they disliked on a piece of pottery. If enough people chose someone, he had to leave Athens for a period of ten years.

FAMOUS PHILOSOPHERS

THALES C. 624–546 BC

Theory: the universe is made of water

SOCRATES C. 469–399 BC

Theory: people should try to live a good life

DEMOCRITUS C. 460–370 BC

Theory: the universe is made of tiny building blocks called atoms

PLATO C. 428–347 BC

Theory: philosophers should rule

ARISTOTLE 384–322 BC

Theory: living in a society with others is mankind's natural state

500–1BC THE CLASSICAL WORLD

This era is called the classical period in Greece and Rome, when their art and culture flourished. Other empires also appeared which united large parts of the world. The Han Empire in China, the Mauryan Empire in India and the Roman Empire in Europe fought off attackers from outside for centuries. Their enormous wealth allowed them to produce beautiful art, such as the terracotta warriors which accompanied a Chinese emperor in his tomb.

218 BC: HANNIBAL

The Carthaginian general Hannibal crosses the Alps into Italy with an army that includes war elephants, beginning the Second Punic War between Rome and Carthage. Rome eventually defeats their Mediterranean rival.

C. 300 BC: MAYAN CAPITAL

The city of Tikal begins to develop with the building of temples. It becomes a major centre of the Maya people as they create city states throughout southern Mexico and Guatemala.

ROME

480 BC: BATTLE OF THERMOPYLAE

King Leonidas and 300 soldiers from the Greek state of Sparta die defending the Pass of Thermopylae against a Persian invading army. They buy enough time to help Sparta's Athenian allies drive the Persians from Greece.

π
DID YOU KNOW?

Archimedes was a Greek maths genius and one of the greatest scientists of the classical world. In 250 BC he was the first person to calculate pi (the ratio of the circumference of a circle to its diameter) almost completely accurately.

C. 100 BC: NAZCA LINES

The Nazca people of Peru start to make geoglyphs – huge lines in the sand representing animals such as snakes and birds – which can only be seen from the air.

KEY EVENT: THE TERRACOTTA ARMY

Having united China in 221 BC by conquering the rest of the Warring States, Qin Shi Huang, the ruler of the kingdom of Qin, declared himself the first emperor of a united China. He had books with records of previous dynasties burned. When he died he was buried in a huge tomb containing over 8,000 life-size terracotta warriors, with horses, chariots and real weapons to guard him in the afterlife. They were only rediscovered in 1974.

44 BC: JULIUS CAESAR

Having been declared dictator for life of the Roman Republic, Julius Caesar is assassinated by a group which fears he wants to make himself king.

220 BC: GREAT WALL OF CHINA

Chinese emperors begin to build a system of walls and towers to defend against nomads beyond their borders. This will eventually develop into the Great Wall of China.

THERMOPYLAE

ISSUS

INDIA

202 BC: HAN DYNASTY

Liu Bang, a peasant who became a rebel leader, is the first emperor of the Han Dynasty. His successors rule China for the next 400 years.

200 BC: POLYNESIAN EXPLORERS

The Polynesian people begin a great migration east of Samoa, which will eventually result in them colonising Hawaii, Rapa Nui (Easter Island) and New Zealand.

262 BC: PILLARS OF ASHOKA

The Mauryan ruler Ashoka converts to Buddhism and sets up pillars throughout the Mauryan Empire (modern-day India) inscribed with Buddhist decrees.

333 BC: ALEXANDER THE GREAT

Alexander the Great, king of Macedon, defeats the Persians at Issus. Within six years he conquers the rest of the Persian Empire and invades India.

NEW ZEALAND

1BC–AD 500 FALL OF EMPIRES

The empires of the classical age continued to prosper for the first half of this period, although they had to survive revolts, famines and plagues. The Mayan cities of central America also experienced a very unstable period before they recovered. But not all of the great empires could survive. Gradually, pressure from nomadic people along the borders of Han China grew, and it collapsed, to be followed by the once mighty Rome.

AD 122: HADRIAN'S WALL

Roman emperor Hadrian orders the building of a wall to mark the northern boundary of the Roman Empire in Britain. Around 8,000 Roman soldiers are stationed there.

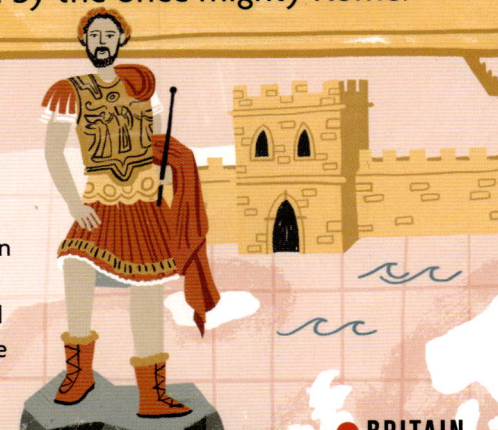

BRITAIN

AD 100: BASKETMAKERS

The Basketmaker people of North America combine hunting and gathering with growing maize and beans and rearing turkeys. They live in villages of shallow-dug pit houses and produce beautifully woven baskets.

AD 80: COLOSSEUM

The Colosseum is completed in Rome. Gladiator fights and beast hunts are held in the amphitheatre, which can seat around 50,000 spectators, and the games to celebrate its opening last 100 days.

ROME

C. AD 30: CHRISTIANITY

The Christian religion begins as followers of Jesus, a preacher from the Middle East who was said to perform miracles, spread his teachings after his death. By AD 380 Christianity is the religion of the Roman Empire.

C. AD 200: TEOTIHUACÁN

Two large pyramids are built in the Mexican city of Teotihuacán, as it expands dramatically. The Pyramid of the Sun is over 65 metres high and is one of ancient Central America's biggest buildings.

NIGERIA

AD 150: NOK CULTURE

The Nok culture (in modern-day Nigeria) reaches its peak; it is the first iron-making culture in West Africa and also produces beautiful ceramics of human heads.

AD 200: MOCHE PEOPLE

The Moche people in northern Peru produce beautiful vases with stirrup-shaped spouts, often in the form of people or animals.

KEY EVENT: THE VANDALS SACK ROME

In AD 286, the Roman Empire was divided into east and west and ruled by two separate emperors, to make it easier to control. But the empire was weakening, attacked by Germanic tribes whom the Romans called barbarians, and in AD 455 a tribe called the Vandals attacked the city of Rome itself. They plundered the city of its treasures and took slaves. They were not the first to sack Rome, but the western empire never recovered from their attack. By AD 476 the last emperor was deposed and the Roman Empire in the west ended.

AD 330: CONSTANTINOPLE

Emperor Constantine establishes Constantinople as the capital for the eastern half of the Roman Empire, later known as the Byzantine Empire. Emperors rule there for a thousand years after the fall of Rome.

CONSTANTINOPLE

AD 220: HAN DYNASTY ENDS

Although Han China manages to defeat the groups of nomads at its northern border, it collapses due to fighting within the royal family.

AD 105: INVENTION OF PAPER

Cai Lun, a court official in China, invents paper by mashing together tree bark and rags. It replaces silk and bamboo as a writing material.

AD 250: YAMATO KINGDOM

The Yamato kingdom emerges in Japan. Its early kings are buried in keyhole-shaped tombs.

AKSUM

VIETNAM

AD 340: AKSUM

The city of Aksum in Ethiopia is an important trading centre for ivory, exotic animals, spices and more. Its kings erect huge stelae (columns) up to 25 metres high and convert to Christianity.

AD 43: TRUNG REBELLION

The Trung sisters lead a revolt against the Han Chinese occupation of Vietnam, but the Han general Ma Yuan crushes it.

DID YOU KNOW?

In AD 132 in China, Zhang Heng built the first known device for detecting earthquakes. When a tremor occurred a pendulum in a bronze jar swung towards one of eight dragon heads fixed on the outside. This then released a metal ball, indicating the direction of the earthquake.

FOCUS ON
ANCIENT ROME
BUILDING AN EMPIRE

There were many large empires in the ancient world, but the Roman Empire was one of the biggest and most powerful. Before 27 BC Rome had been a republic, ruled by the senate, a group of men from important Roman families. They controlled all of Italy and conquered kingdoms around the Mediterranean Sea. But the senators began to fight among themselves, until they lost their power, an emperor took control, and the Roman Empire began.

EMPERORS IN CHARGE

Augustus became Rome's first emperor after defeating his rivals in battle. Emperors usually chose who would take their place after they died, but others became emperor by defeating their rivals. Some were fair rulers, but others were cruel and brutal to their people – Emperor Caligula is remembered for killing anyone who refused to worship him like a god. It was important for all emperors to demonstrate their power and strength, and many did this by growing the empire. It was the brilliant Roman army that made this possible.

A ROMAN LEGIONARY

ROMAN ARMY

The Roman army was the largest in the ancient world, and it was also very well organised. There were two main types of soldiers: legionaries and auxiliaries. Auxiliaries were soldiers who were not Roman citizens, while legionaries were the best of the best – well trained, experienced and with better armour and weapons than their opponents.

The army's discipline and clever tactics made it formidable. Soldiers attacked in tight formations and moved under a roof of shields (known as the "tortoise" formation) so that enemies couldn't hit them with arrows. These tactics helped them conquer territories far and wide.

ROMAN EMPERORS

These are a few of the most memorable Roman emperors – for better or worse!

AUGUSTUS
27 BC–AD14

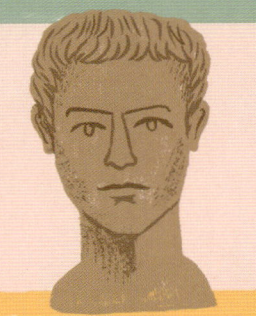

CALIGULA
AD 37–41

CLAUDIUS
AD 41–54

THE TORTOISE FORMATION

MANAGING THE EMPIRE

Roman soldiers had to be fit enough to march huge distances – over 30 kilometres a day – to get across the vast empire. By AD 117, under Emperor Trajan, the Roman Empire was at its largest, stretching as far as Britain to the north and Egypt in the south. Managing such a huge area was difficult, and the Romans built straight, paved roads to make travelling around easier. Even so, getting from one end of the empire to the other could have taken as long as seven weeks. The Romans built forts to defend their borders, and are thought to have had half a million soldiers fighting in their army, but despite all this they eventually struggled to keep control of such a big empire. By AD 286 it was split into an east and west empire.

THE ROMAN EMPIRE
AD 117

N

NERO
AD 54–68

TRAJAN
AD 98–117

HADRIAN
AD 117–138

MARCUS AURELIUS
AD 161–180

500–1000 NEW KINGDOMS

After the collapse of the empires from the classical age, the world moved into a new period. China was reunited once more and new kingdoms appeared, such as Ghana in West Africa and the Khmer in Cambodia. In Europe this period is known as the Middle Ages, during which there were attacks by raiders such as the Vikings from Scandinavia. Despite this, strong kingdoms did manage to develop. The most important of these was Francia, which under the great ruler Charlemagne grew to control a large part of western Europe.

793: VIKINGS

Viking raiders from Scandinavia attack the monastery of Lindisfarne in northern England, beginning a 250-year period in which they plunder and conquer parts of Britain, Ireland and France and establish colonies in Russia, Iceland and Greenland.

LINDISFARNE

GAUL

850: PUEBLO PEOPLE

The Pueblo people of south-west North America build multiple-storey villages, often against cliffs, such as Chaco Canyon.

711: MOOR CONQUEST

A Muslim force crosses into Spain from North Africa and defeats the kingdom of the Visigoths tribe. Known as the Moors, they establish Muslim rule over all except the far north of the country.

683: MAYANS

K'inich Janaab Pakal, the Mayan king also known as Pakal the Great, dies and is buried in a richly decorated sarcophagus in the Temple of the Inscriptions. During his 68-year reign over the city state of Palenque, he had constructed many incredible buildings. By the 800s Palenque and other Mayan cities are abandoned, for reasons which remain mysterious.

C. 700: KINGDOM OF GHANA

The kingdom of Ghana emerges on the southern fringes of the Sahara desert. It grows rich trading salt, gold, ivory and slaves.

DID YOU KNOW?

For three hundred years from around 858, Japan was ruled by child emperors. They were controlled by members of the Fujiwara clan who acted as "regents" to the children and made decisions for them. Once the child reached adulthood, they were forced to step down.

KEY EVENT: THE CORONATION OF CHARLEMAGNE

Charlemagne had been king of the Franks, or Francia, an area of Europe covering much of modern-day France and Germany, since his father died in 768. He set about expanding his kingdom in Europe until on Christmas Day 800 in Rome, Pope Leo III crowned Charlemagne emperor of the Romans. This was the beginning of the Holy Roman Empire, which ruled over Germany until 1806. Charlemagne himself conquered parts of northern Spain, Germany, Austria and Italy and became Europe's most powerful ruler until his death in 814.

507: CLOVIS

Clovis, the first king to unite all the tribes of Franks, defeats the Visigoth tribe in Gaul. This expands his kingdom further into what will later become France.

618: SILK ROAD

Li Yuan, a military governor in China, defeats rebels and declares himself Emperor Gaozu, first emperor of the Tang Dynasty. It's the beginning of a period of prosperity and trade flowing along the Silk Road to the west.

936: KOREA UNITED

Wang Kon, the ruler of the north Korean state of Goguryeo, conquers the rival kingdoms of Baekche and Silla, reuniting Korea and starting a dynasty that will rule until 1392.

KOREA

762: ISLAMIC EMPIRE

The caliph (Muslim ruler) al-Mansur founds the Round City of Baghdad as a capital for the Islamic Empire. It becomes a centre of learning and science, and for merchants from as far afield as Europe and China.

622: HEGIRA

The prophet Muhammad, founder of the Muslim religion, flees with his followers from Mecca, where they were being persecuted, to Medina, where local tribes welcome them. Their journey is known as the Hegira.

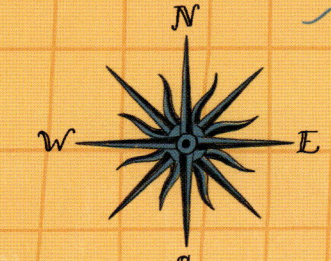

802: KHMER KINGDOM

The Cambodian king Jayavarman II declares himself a cakravartin ("universal lord"), founding the Khmer kingdom. His successors build spectacular temples.

N
W   E
S

FOCUS ON
CHINA
THE SILK ROAD

Chinese merchants had travelled west to trade precious goods such as silk with Persia and the Roman Empire since the time of the Han Dynasty. They used a series of routes which together became known as the Silk Road, and they brought back with them great wealth and new ideas. During the Tang Dynasty especially trade flourished along the 6,500-kilometre length of the Silk Road controlled by China. When China lost control of the routes in the 1300s, the Silk Road fell into disuse.

BUILDING THE SILK ROAD

Around 140 BC, the Han emperor of China sent an expedition to explore lands to the west. It found rich kingdoms with which China could trade and merchants began to follow in its footsteps. The trade in silk grew so valuable that nomads started attacking trading caravans to steal the goods and cash they carried. The Chinese emperors sent armies to stop them and set up forts to guard the Silk Road. By about 30 BC they occupied most of its eastern part, so merchants could travel safely.

Rome
Petra
PERSIA
AFRICA
W

TRAVELLERS AND IDEAS

As well as trade, merchants on the Silk Road brought with them ideas, such as knowledge of paper and gunpowder which the Chinese invented. In the same way, the Buddhist religion, which had developed in India, spread east into China. Travellers such as the Venetian merchant Marco Polo were also able to use the Silk Road to visit China. After he returned home in 1295, Polo composed an account of his experiences, which gave Europeans a better understanding of China and its culture.

SILK ROAD TOWNS

The Silk Road began at Chang'an, the Chinese capital. It became very rich from the trade and by 800 was the largest city in the world. A lot of the Silk Road passed through very difficult territory such as deserts and the merchants stopped in oases, which were places where they could find food and shelter. Under Chinese rule these grew into prosperous towns, where people from many different countries met, traded goods and exchanged ideas. Splendid Buddhist shrines were built along the Silk Road, such as at Dunhuang where Buddhist images were painted on cave walls and religious books were composed, including the Diamond Sutra, the world's first printed book. Oasis towns like Kashgar remained important for centuries.

Kashgar

Dunhuang

Chang'an

CHINA

INDIA

ITEMS TRADED ON THE SILK ROAD

SILK

The Silk Road's most famous trading item, silk, was valued in the west for the fine clothing fabric it could make. The Chinese kept knowledge of the silkworms which were needed to create it a secret for centuries.

TEA

Tea was first grown in China and Chinese merchants spread knowledge of the drink as they travelled.

PAPER

The Chinese invented paper in 105, and gradually it replaced the parchment made of animal skins or papyrus made from reeds which were used in the Middle East and Europe.

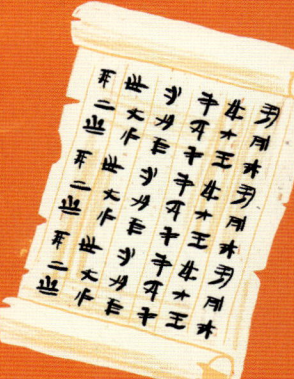

GLASS

The Chinese did not know how to blow glass or how to make clear glass, so they imported it along the Silk Road.

SILVER

Many of the goods bought from Chinese merchants were paid for in silver and so huge quantities of this travelled back east.

PORCELAIN

The Chinese invented porcelain, a type of fine white pottery that was very strong and became one of China's most popular exports.

1000–1300 THE AGE OF WARRIORS

As the Middle Ages continued, a new force made its mark on the world: in the 1200s the Mongols, fierce horse-borne nomads, attacked west and south from the plains of central Asia, building the largest continuous empire of all time. This period is also known for the struggle between newly powerful Christian rulers and the Muslim world, as armies of Christian crusaders were sent to claim Jerusalem and the rest of the Holy Land from its Islamic rulers.

1066: BATTLE OF HASTINGS

Duke William of Normandy invades England and defeats King Harold in a battle at Hastings. William takes over as king, beginning Norman rule in England when castles are built throughout the country.

ENGLAND

C. 1100: MISSISSIPPI CULTURE

Cahokia, the main settlement of the Mississippian culture in North America, is home to 20,000 people. The city has over 100 platform mounds with buildings on top, and it is at the centre of trading networks.

1212: RECONQUISTA

Christian forces defeat the Muslim army led by Sultan Muhammad al-Nasir in a crucial battle in the Reconquista, the campaign to recapture Spain from Muslim rulers. By 1250 only Granada remains under Muslim control.

1088: FIRST EUROPEAN UNIVERSITY

The first university in Europe is founded at Bologna, and similar institutions spread throughout Italy and France. At first they train lawyers in church law, but gradually begin to teach more subjects, including studying ancient Greek and Roman authors. The first university in the world was founded in Morocco by Fatima al-Fihri in 859.

C. 1200: CHIMÚ PEOPLE

The city of Chan Chan, the capital of the Chimú people in Peru, has 40,000 inhabitants. It is divided into a series of walled compounds, each built by successive Chimú kings.

C. 1200: GREAT ZIMBABWE

The city of Great Zimbabwe is constructed as the main centre for the Zimbabwe kingdom of southern Africa. It grows wealthy trading gold and ivory and its 11-metre high walls provide shelter for more than 10,000 people.

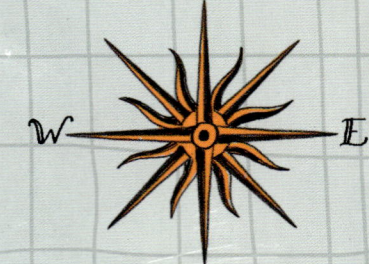

KEY EVENT: BATTLE OF HATTIN

In 1095 the Pope called for Christians to capture Jerusalem, which had been out of their control for centuries, in a holy war later known as a Crusade. Thousands of men in Europe answered his call and four years later, the crusader army seized Jerusalem and set up a series of crusader-ruled states in Palestine and Syria. Gradually, local Muslim rulers fought back, recapturing some of the land. Finally, in 1187, Saladin, the sultan of Egypt, destroyed the main crusader army at the Horns of Hattin, in modern Israel. He then swept down and captured Jerusalem, which had been left virtually defenceless. The shock of the loss of their holiest city was enormous for the Christian rulers of Europe and they launched another Crusade. Despite a number of victories, it failed to retake Jerusalem. Although Crusades continued into the 1400s, by 1291 the crusaders had been expelled from the Holy Land.

DID YOU KNOW?

In 1232 the first military use of rockets was recorded, when Chinese troops defending a town against a Mongol attack used "flying-fire arrows". They stuffed gunpowder into bamboo tubes and when lit, the gunpowder shot primitive rockets towards the Mongol lines. They were very inaccurate but made enough fire and noise to scare the Mongols into retreating.

1204: SACKING OF CONSTANTINOPLE

The army of the Fourth Crusade sacks Constantinople and takes over the Byzantine Empire, which is ruled by Latin (western European) emperors until the Byzantines recover it in 1261.

1206: GENGHIS KHAN

Temujin, a Mongol warrior, is declared Genghis Khan, leader of the Mongol peoples of central Asia. He unites and organises the Mongol tribes into an effective fighting force and conquers neighbouring powers, including China and Persia. Genghis Khan conquers more land than anyone else in history.

1192: FIRST SHOGUN

Minamoto Yoritomo becomes the first shogun (military dictator) of Japan, after his clan wins the Genpei War against its Taira rivals.

1279: MONGOL DYNASTY

The Mongol army of Kublai Khan (grandson of Genghis) conquers China. The Mongol Yuan Dynasty rules the whole country.

INDIA

1113: ANGKOR WAT

Suryavarman II, ruler of the Khmer kingdom, builds the massive Angkor Wat temple in Cambodia.

1175: SULTANS OF DELHI

Muhammad of Ghur (modern Afghanistan) invades northern India, which leads to the beginning of the sultanate of Delhi – a series of Muslim kings who rule the region for over 300 years. They build monuments like the Qutb Minar tower to mark their victories.

C. 1250: MAORI

The Maori people sail south and east from Polynesia in canoes and settle in New Zealand, one of the last large uninhabited parts of the world. They build pa (forts) as warfare breaks out among tribes.

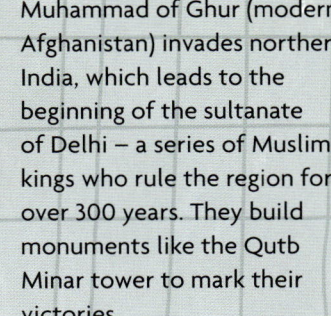

NEW ZEALAND

1300–1450
NEW BEGINNINGS

There was a cultural and scientific revolution in Europe at this time, called the Renaissance, which began in Italy. In Asia, the Mongols lost much of their power, as the Ming Dynasty overthrew them in China and soon grew powerful. Elsewhere, new empires were founded, including the Inca in Peru, the Aztec in Mexico, and the Ottoman Empire, which conquered most of modern Turkey and parts of south-eastern Europe. But it was the Mali Empire in West Africa that could boast unimaginable riches.

1325: AZTECS
The Aztecs build their capital at Tenochtitlán in central Mexico. They are fierce warriors and by 1434 rule a great empire.

1429: JOAN OF ARC
Joan of Arc, a teenage peasant, leads the French army to lift a siege of Orléans during the Hundred Years' War between England and France. She is captured and burnt at the stake by the English in 1431.

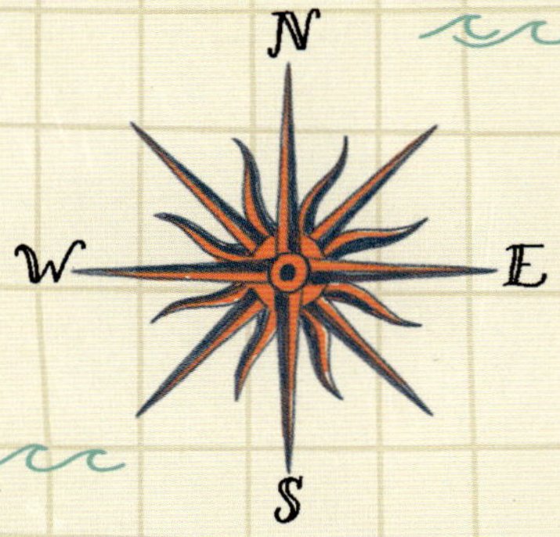

FLORENCE

1436: RENAISSANCE
The architect and engineer Filippo Brunelleschi completes the huge dome of Florence cathedral in Italy. It is a key achievement in the Renaissance, a movement of artistic and cultural renewal in Europe inspired by interest in the works of the ancient Greeks and Romans.

1438: INCAS
Pachacuti Inca Yupanqui becomes ruler of the Incas, a mountain people in Peru. He sets out to create a huge Incan empire, rapidly gaining land further south, laying out the capital city at Cusco and building a great stone fortress at Sacsayhuamán, and the spectacular town of Machu Picchu, hidden high in the Andes.

DID YOU KNOW?
By 1300 the people of Rapa Nui (Easter Island) in the Pacific Ocean had begun carving almost a thousand huge statues up to 10 metres high and 80 tonnes in weight, known as moai. They set them up facing out to sea and it is thought they represent ancestral spirits.

KEY EVENT:
THE PILGRIMAGE OF MANSA MUSA

Mali was the largest empire in West Africa, and earned a lot of its wealth from its gold mines. In 1324, its ruler Mansa Musa set out on a pilgrimage to Mecca. But unlike others making this journey, Mansa Musa's travelling party included 60,000 men and 80 camels laden with bags full of gold – for Mansa Musa is thought to be the richest man who ever lived. When his party reached Cairo, their spending was so lavish that it damaged the local economy. When Mansa Musa returned to Mali he ordered the building of a mosque and Islamic school at Timbuktu, which developed into a university.

1346: BLACK DEATH

The Black Death, a highly infectious plague, breaks out in Crimea and is carried by merchant ships to Italy and then spreads throughout Europe. The disease causes sufferers' skin to break out in black boils and kills over a third of the population of Europe and huge numbers in China and the Middle East – more than any other pandemic in history so far.

1402: TIMUR

The Ottoman Empire, founded around 1300, almost breaks apart after a major defeat by the mighty Mongol warlord Timur at Ankara. The Ottomans recover and grow stronger, while Timur's empire collapses a few years later.

1406: FORBIDDEN CITY

The Chinese Ming emperor Yongle orders the construction of the Forbidden City, a lavish palace complex in Beijing which has over 8,000 rooms.

KOREA

1446: KOREAN ALPHABET

A new Korean alphabet is created by King Sejong, called the Hangul.

VIETNAM

1336: VIJAYANAGAR EMPIRE

The Hindu empire of Vijayanagar is founded after a revolt against the Muslim rulers of Delhi. It becomes the strongest kingdom in south India for the next 300 years and builds impressive temples.

1428: DAI VIET KINGDOM

Le Loi, a wealthy landowner, expels the Chinese from Vietnam after a 20-year occupation and restores the Dai Viet kingdom.

1414: MING VOYAGES

The Chinese admiral Zheng He reaches Malindi on the east coast of Africa during his fourth voyage of exploration. He brings back a giraffe to the Ming emperor Yongle. Zheng completes seven voyages in total, with fleets of huge "treasure ships" that carry Chinese influence throughout the Indian Ocean.

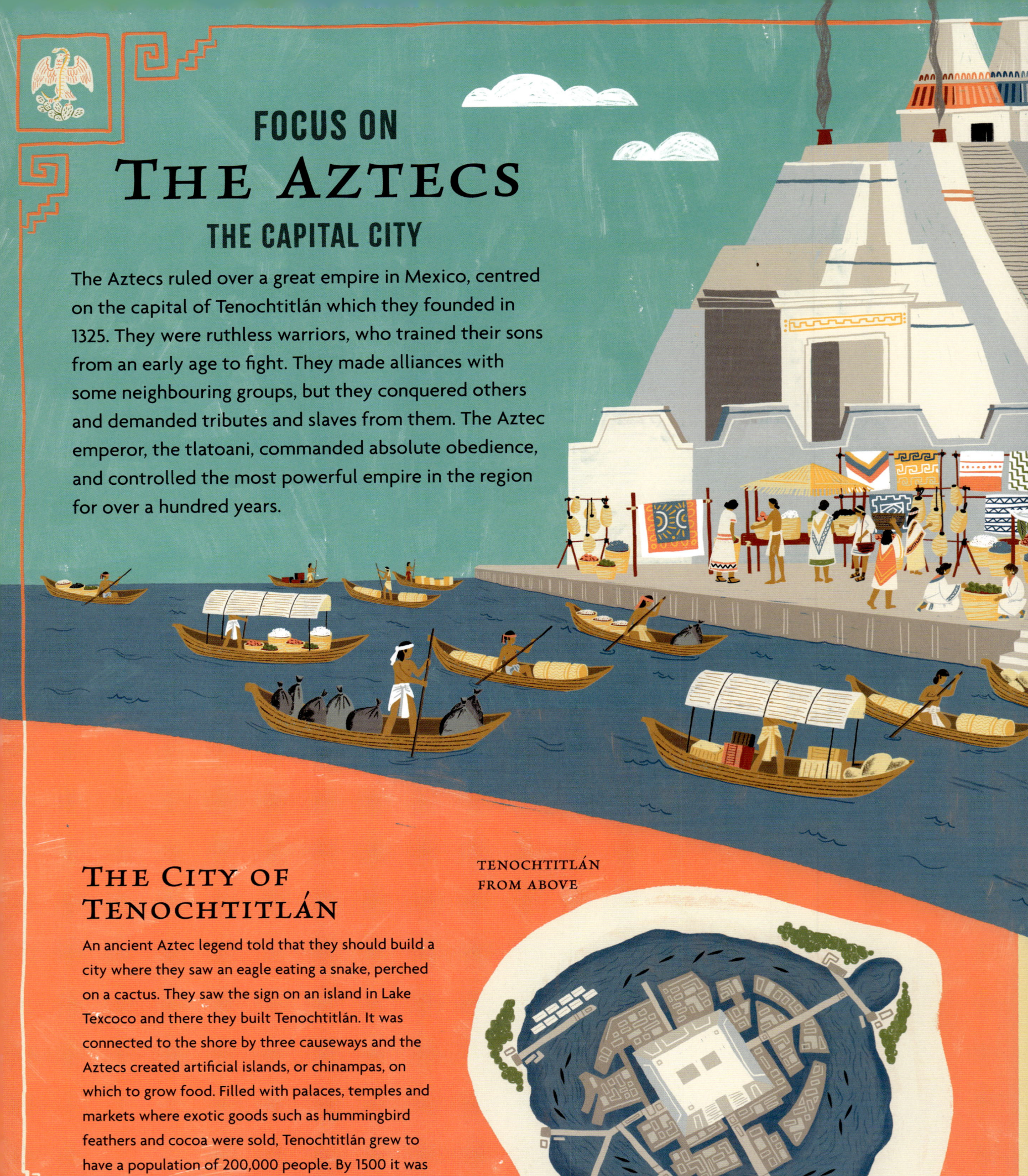

FOCUS ON
THE AZTECS
THE CAPITAL CITY

The Aztecs ruled over a great empire in Mexico, centred on the capital of Tenochtitlán which they founded in 1325. They were ruthless warriors, who trained their sons from an early age to fight. They made alliances with some neighbouring groups, but they conquered others and demanded tributes and slaves from them. The Aztec emperor, the tlatoani, commanded absolute obedience, and controlled the most powerful empire in the region for over a hundred years.

THE CITY OF TENOCHTITLÁN

An ancient Aztec legend told that they should build a city where they saw an eagle eating a snake, perched on a cactus. They saw the sign on an island in Lake Texcoco and there they built Tenochtitlán. It was connected to the shore by three causeways and the Aztecs created artificial islands, or chinampas, on which to grow food. Filled with palaces, temples and markets where exotic goods such as hummingbird feathers and cocoa were sold, Tenochtitlán grew to have a population of 200,000 people. By 1500 it was one of the largest cities in the world.

TENOCHTITLÁN
FROM ABOVE

AZTEC GODS

TONATIUH

Known as "he who goes forth shining", Tonatiuh was the god of the Sun. Special sacrifices were made to him at the coronation of Aztec emperors.

TEZCATLIPOCA

"The smoking mirror" was the supreme god and guardian of the Aztec emperors. He carried an obsidian mirror in which he could see everything that took place in the world, and a quiver of arrows to punish wrongdoers.

QUETZALCOATL

"The feathered serpent" was the god of wind, thunder and knowledge, and the special patron of priests. When Spanish conquerors arrived in 1519, the Aztecs at first thought their leader Hernán Cortés was the god returning to Mexico.

HUITZILOPOCHTLI

"The hummingbird on the left" was the god of war who demanded a constant stream of sacrificial victims to stop him from becoming angry.

TLALOC

Tlaloc was the rain god. The Aztecs needed to keep him happy so that he would send rain, without which the maize they needed for food would die.

XIPE TOTEC

The flayed god was a fertility god to whom special sacrifices were made. The victims' skin was removed, prepared and then worn by Xipe Totec's priests as a cloak.

TEMPLES AND SACRIFICES

At the heart of Tenochtitlán was the Templo Mayor, the city's largest temple, in the form of a massive pyramid with stairs leading to the top. There, Aztec priests sacrificed captives by cutting their heart out with a sharp obsidian knife. They believed the victims' blood repaid the gods for the blood they had shed when creating the world. The Aztecs worshipped hundreds of gods but some were more significant than others.

27

1450-1550 A TIME OF CHANGE

This is a century of enormous change. European explorers began to reach the Americas, disrupting and often destroying the civilisations there. Christopher Columbus landed in the Bahamas, and soon after the Spanish conquered the Aztec and Inca empires. Meanwhile, the great Muslim empires – the Safavids, Ottomans and Mughals – grew in strength, but Christianity in western Europe split into two camps and religious wars broke out between them. This was the Reformation, triggered by the German monk Martin Luther questioning the beliefs of the Catholic Church.

1535: FRENCH EXPEDITION

A French expedition led by Jacques Cartier explores the coast and rivers of Canada. He reaches the village of Hochelaga, the future Montréal, and claims land for France.

1534: HENRY VIII

King Henry VIII makes himself head of a new Church of England after the Pope refuses to let him divorce his first wife, Catherine of Aragon. By the time he dies in 1547, Henry has married six times.

GERMAN

ITALY

1519: DESTRUCTION OF THE AZTEC EMPIRE

The Spanish explorer Hernán Cortés arrives in Mexico. He gathers allies among the tribes who have warred with the powerful Aztecs, and whose people have been sacrificed at their Templo Mayor. The Spanish then capture and destroy Tenochtitlán and end the Aztec Empire.

1492: CHRISTOPHER COLUMBUS

Italian captain Christopher Columbus crosses the Atlantic and lands on the island of Guanahani in the Bahamas. He believes that he has found East Asia, but has in fact reached the Americas.

1532: SPANISH INVASION

The powerful Inca Empire in Peru has been weakened by civil war and disease. When a tiny force of Spanish conquistadors (soldiers) arrive and capture its ruler, it collapses.

C. 1550: KINGDOM OF BENIN

Orhogbua, the oba (ruler) of Benin, conquers much of his neighbours' territories in West Africa, turning Benin into a wealthy empire. Craftsmen in the capital, Benin City, make elaborate heads out of bronze.

DID YOU KNOW?

At this time, most people believed the Earth was the centre of the universe. In 1543 Polish astronomer Nicolaus Copernicus challenged this by publishing his theory that the Earth orbits around the Sun.

KEY EVENT: LUTHER'S 95 THESES

By the 1500s, some people in Europe had begun to criticise the Catholic Church as being corrupt. The German monk Martin Luther wrote 95 theses that questioned certain practices of the Catholic Church, such as the sale of indulgences, certificates which forgave the buyer's sins. He nailed them on the door of the church at Wittenberg in Saxony on 31 October 1517. Luther's ideas soon spread and found many followers and the Pope excommunicated him (cut him off from membership of the Church). Many German princes took up Luther's cause, sparking a religious war with the Catholic Holy Roman emperor Charles V. The movement of religious change Luther started became known as the Reformation and his followers were called Protestants, who rejected the authority of the Pope and many Catholic beliefs.

1450: PRINTING PRESS

Johannes Gutenberg invents a printing press in Germany that allows books to be mass-produced rather than copied by hand. This makes it easier for learning and new ideas to spread around the world.

1547: IVAN THE TERRIBLE

Ivan IV becomes the first Tsar of Russia. He conquers territory in central Asia and clamps down on the boyars, a class of warrior nobles, with such savagery that he gains the nickname "the Terrible".

C. 1503: MONA LISA

The Italian Leonardo da Vinci paints the Mona Lisa. It is one of the masterpieces of Renaissance art, created by a genius who also draws versions of helicopters centuries before their invention.

1453: FALL OF CONSTANTINOPLE

The Ottomans capture Constantinople, capital of the Byzantine Empire. They turn many of its churches, including Hagia Sophia, into mosques. The Byzantine Empire collapses.

1526: MUGHAL EMPIRE

Babur, a descendent of Genghis Khan, captures Delhi and unites most of northern India under his rule as the first Mughal emperor.

1498: SPICE TRADE

The Portuguese explorer Vasco da Gama sails from Europe, up the east coast of Africa and arrives in India. This opens up a new sea route for European trade in valuable spices such as pepper and nutmeg.

29

1550-1650
EXPANDING HORIZONS

This was a time of new scientific advances, as people started to experiment and observe in physics, astronomy, chemistry and medicine, instead of relying on old beliefs. While India, Japan and China were unified and enjoying a flourishing culture in Asia, Europe suffered devastating religious wars. Even so, Europeans continued to explore the globe, and reached Australia. Some began to colonise North America, including those such as the Pilgrim Fathers who were seeking freedom to practise their religion.

KEY EVENT: PILGRIMS LAND IN AMERICA

On 9 November 1620 a ship called the Mayflower carrying 102 passengers, many of them fleeing from religious persecution in England, arrived off the coast of Massachusetts. Many of them died during a first, harsh winter but some survived thanks to help from the local Wampanoag tribe. Later known as the Pilgrim Fathers, the settlers grew in number and in 1630 founded Boston. They weren't the first European settlers, but are well known for the Thanksgiving feast they shared with the Wampanoag.

1607: ENGLISH SETTLEMENT

The first permanent English settlement in North America is established at Jamestown, Virginia. Many colonists die of disease and starvation, until more settlers bring supplies and they start to grow and trade tobacco. The diseases Europeans unknowingly bring with them kill many Native Americans and a war breaks out between the Powhatan people and the Jamestown settlers, the first of many American-Indian wars as the settlers begin to take their land.

ENGLAND

1606: WILLIAM SHAKESPEARE

William Shakespeare's play *Macbeth* is first performed. The greatest English playwright, Shakespeare writes around 40 plays, including tragedies, comedies and dramas which deal with the history of England.

1610: GALILEO

Italian astronomer Galileo Galilei uses the recently invented telescope to help prove Copernicus's theory that the Earth orbits around the Sun. He is tried for heresy (going against religion) by the Catholic Church.

DID YOU KNOW?

Going to the toilet used to be a messy business in England, involving a chamber pot which had to be emptied out by hand. In 1596 Sir John Harington solved this problem by inventing the first flush toilet, in which water swept the contents into a pit. He called it the Ajax and presented one to Queen Elizabeth I, but she didn't like it and so the idea did not catch on for another 200 years, and it was another 100 years after that before toilet roll was invented.

1572: END OF THE INCAS

The Spanish capture the city of Vilcabamba, where the last Inca emperor, Tupac Amaru, has been holding out against them. This completes their conquest of Peru.

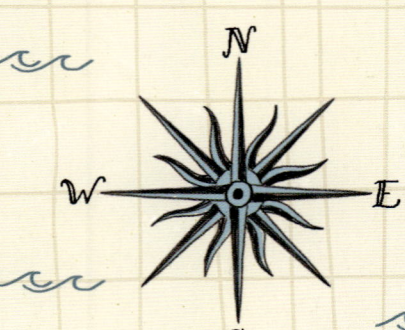

1620: THIRTY YEARS' WAR

A Protestant army is defeated by the Holy Roman emperor Ferdinand II at the first battle of the Thirty Years' War. The war pits Catholic Spain and Austria against largely Protestant states including Sweden and the Netherlands.

ITALY

1613: ROMANOV DYNASTY

Mikhail Romanov is elected Tsar of Russia, ending a period of civil war and famine. His dynasty, the Romanovs, rule Russia until 1917.

1644: QING DYNASTY

Rebels seize Beijing and depose the last Ming emperor of China. Months later, Manchu tribesmen from north-east Asia capture the city and install a six-year-old as emperor, and conquer the rest of China by 1681. They force Manchu customs on the Chinese, such as the wearing of the "queue", a long plait, for men. This is the start of the Qing Dynasty.

1632: TAJ MAHAL

The Mughal emperor Shah Jahan begins construction of the Taj Mahal in India, a tomb for his beloved wife Mumtaz Mahal. It takes eleven years to build.

1598: SAFAVID CAPITAL

The Safavid Empire, covering modern-day Iran, builds a new capital at Isfahan. The ruler, Shah Abbas, creates the Maidan, one of the most beautiful city squares in the world.

1603: EDO PERIOD

Tokugawa Ieyasu becomes shogun of Japan, ending a 150-year civil war. The Tokugawa shoguns rule until 1868, and during most of this time, known as the Edo Period, Japan bans citizens from leaving and foreigners from entering.

1636: ETHIOPIAN EMPIRE

The Ethiopian emperor Fasilides builds a new capital at Gondar, including a palace, library, royal tombs and a fortress. This is the first capital city of the empire since it began in 1270. Previously its emperors had stayed in royal camps that moved often.

1642: MAORI MEETING

The Dutch explorer Abel Tasman lands on what is now Tasmania before sailing on to New Zealand's South Island, where he comes in contact with local Maori.

1619: DUTCH EAST INDIA COMPANY

The powerful Dutch East India Company conquers a city in Java to establish its headquarters there. It dominates the trade in spices and rules much of Indonesia. Its rival is the English East India Company, which has its main bases in India.

TASMANIA

FOCUS ON
JAPAN
EDO PERIOD

By the 1500s Japan was no longer a united country. The emperors who had once ruled it had lost power and shoguns (military dictators) governed in their place. Warlords called daimyos fought over the country with their bands of samurai warriors. In 1603 one of them, Tokugawa Ieyasu, defeated the rest, ending the wars and uniting Japan once more. His family, the Tokugawa, ruled Japan as shoguns for the next 250 years in the Edo Period, bringing peace and allowing Japanese culture to flourish.

SHOGUNS

Originally Japanese emperors gave the title shogun to their top military generals. But in 1192 the shogun Minamoto Yoritomo took power for himself, and for nearly 700 years the emperors were powerless as various daimyo families occupied the shogunate. When the Tokugawa family took over, they kept Japan isolated from the rest of the world, banning foreigners from entering for two centuries. The Tokugawa shoguns enforced strict rules separating the daimyo and samurai class from the merchants, artisans and peasants.

SAMURAI

The samurai were a class of elite warriors who first appeared in the 900s. They wore elaborate armour, with large crests on the helmet representing their family. They were experts with the bow, but their most famous weapon was the katana, a razor-sharp curved steel sword.

FAMOUS SAMURAI AND SHOGUNS

Many samurai and shoguns throughout Japanese history won fame for their deeds. Some fought heroically in battle, others died rather than be dishonoured and others helped reunify the country.

MINAMOTO NO YOSHITSUNE (1159–1189)

won an earlier civil war in Japan and in 1192 helped his half-brother become the first ruling shogun.

KUSONOKI MASAHIGE (1294–1336)

was a samurai who, rather than disobey the emperor, marched his forces to certain death against a far larger army.

Samurai pledged loyalty to a daimyo lord, but they had a strong code of honour, called bushido, and many chose to commit suicide rather than surrender in battle or perform what they saw as dishonourable acts.

TOKUGAWA SOCIETY

The Tokugawa shoguns were able to keep tight control over their country by isolating it from the rest of the world. This also allowed a distinctive culture to develop in Japan, and arts flourished in the capital Edo (modern Tokyo). Noh, a style of dance drama using elaborate masks and costumes to tell traditional tales, was popular among the daimyo, while kabuki theatre, which allowed female actors, was more sought after by commoners. Ukiyo-e, a style of woodblock printing which showed landscapes and often kabuki actors, also flourished under the Tokugawa.

ODA NOBUNAGA (1534–1582)
was a daimyo who began the reunification of Japan, but died before he could complete it.

TOKUGAWA IEYASU (1543–1616)
was an ally of Oda Nobunaga. He defeated the last independent warlords and in 1603 declared himself shogun, the ruler of a united Japan.

SANADA YUKIMURA (1567–1615)
was a samurai who heroically defended Osaka castle against the Tokugawa army in 1615, but died in the final attack.

1650–1750 THE AGE OF ENLIGHTENMENT

This period saw changing fortunes for the empires and dynasties of Asia. Under the new Qing Dynasty, China conquered new territories, but the main Muslim empires – the Ottomans, Safavids and Mughals – all went into decline. Meanwhile in Europe, kings such as Louis XIV in France and Russia's Peter the Great claimed absolute power over their subjects and enlarged their kingdoms. In Europe, people began challenging traditional ways of thinking about the world and publishing many new ideas, in a time known as the Enlightenment. There were many advances and new discoveries in science and philosophy, including Isaac Newton's theory of gravity.

1692: WITCH TRIALS

A witch-hunting craze grips the Massachusetts town of Salem in America. Many people are forced into confessing to being witches in a series of trials and fourteen women (mostly young) and five men are hanged.

1666: GREAT FIRE

The Great Fire of London begins in a baker's shop and burns for five days, destroying much of the centre of England's capital city.

● LONDON

1661: SUN KING

The French king Louis XIV begins work on a new palace at Versailles, near Paris. The splendour of the court there gives Louis the nickname "the Sun King". France grows powerful under his reign.

1692: EARTHQUAKE

A massive earthquake hits Port Royal in Jamaica, a notorious haven for pirates. Five thousand people are killed and the port sinks beneath the Caribbean Sea.

1750: SLAVE TRADE

The Atlantic slave trade is at its height. Hundreds of European ships each year carry people captured in Africa across the Atlantic to work in appalling conditions on plantations from Brazil to the Caribbean and North America. Many die during the crossing and it is estimated in total around 12 million Africans are taken as slaves over the course of more than 300 years.

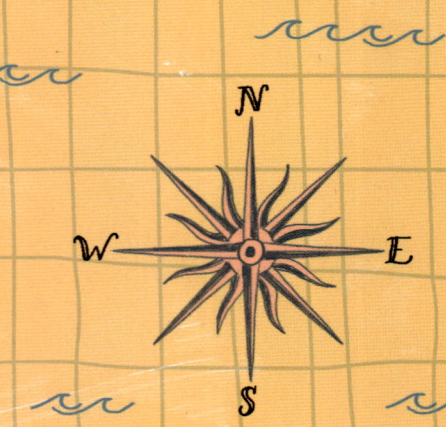

1701: ASANTE EMPIRE

Osei Kofi Tutu is crowned king of all the Asante people. The Asante Empire, in modern-day Ghana, dominates trade with Europeans and blocks European expansion into parts of Africa until the late 1800s.

1652: CAPE TOWN

A Dutch expedition establishes Cape Town, the first European settlement in southern Africa. It is a supply base for Dutch East India Company ships travelling to the spice islands of Indonesia.

KEY EVENT: DISCOVERING GRAVITY

Legend has it that the English mathematician Isaac Newton had his revolutionary idea when he was sitting under a tree and an apple fell on his head. He realised that an unseen force was attracting the apple to the Earth, and this inspired him to put forward his theory of gravity. He extended this idea to explain that it was the Sun's gravitational pull that makes the planets orbit around it. One of the key thinkers of the Enlightenment, Newton revolutionised physics when he published his theory in the *Philosophiæ Naturalis Principia Mathematica* ("The Mathematical Principles of Natural Philosophy") in 1687.

DID YOU KNOW?

The tiny cells that make up all living things were named by the English scientist Robert Hooke in 1665 when he observed them through his newly invented microscope. He also studied snowflakes, insects and more.

ST PETERSBURG

1703: PETER THE GREAT

Tsar Peter the Great establishes a new capital city at St Petersburg. It is part of his efforts to modernise Russia by reforming its government, economy and farms. In 1721 the Russian Empire is created.

CHINA

1683: QING EMPIRE

Kangxi, the longest ruling Chinese emperor in history, crushes revolutions until his Qing Dynasty controls the whole of China. In 1683 he expands his empire by capturing Taiwan, defeating a group loyal to the old Ming Dynasty.

1736: SAFAVID DYNASTY

Nader Shah overthrows the last ruler of the weakened Safavid Dynasty and declares himself Shah of Iran. A powerful ruler, he captures Delhi, where the Mughal emperor has to persuade him to leave by giving him treasures including the Peacock Throne.

1707: MUGHAL EMPIRE DECLINES

Aurangzeb, the last great Mughal emperor, dies. The empire rapidly shrinks until it controls only the region around Delhi.

C. 1690: DEATH OF THE DODO

The dodo, a flightless bird on the island of Mauritius, becomes extinct, after passing European sailors hunt it for meat and rats which escape from their ships kill the rest.

FOCUS ON
MUGHAL INDIA
ART AND BUILDINGS

In 1526 a warlord from central Asia named Babur founded the Mughal Empire when he invaded northern India and defeated the Sultan of Delhi. His descendants extended Mughal rule, and by 1700 they had conquered almost the whole of India. Their court was a glittering place, as they encouraged poets and painters and built spectacular mosques, palaces and tombs. However, in the 1700s they faced revolts from groups such as the Marathas, while Europeans, in particular the British, also occupied more and more of India. By the time the last Mughal emperor was deposed in 1857, he ruled only a small area in Delhi and had little of the power and wealth the empire had once enjoyed.

MUGHAL ART

The Mughal emperors were great supporters of the arts. Emperor Akbar set up a workshop in the 1500s where artists painted a style of miniature pictures that originally came from Persia, and this tradition continued under later emperors. Many of the miniatures were used to illustrate books containing history or epic tales. The Mughals also encouraged music, employing court musicians, and poetry. Bahadur Shah, the very last Mughal emperor, was himself an accomplished poet.

MUGHAL BUILDINGS

The Mughals developed a blend of Turkish, Persian and Indian styles to construct splendid buildings throughout their empire, including forts, tombs, palaces, mosques and gardens.

HUMAYUN'S TOMB, DELHI

THE RED FORT, DELHI

AKBAR THE GREAT

Akbar ruled for nearly 50 years until his death in 1605. He grew the empire and built a splendid new capital at Fatehpur Sikri. Although a Muslim, he was tolerant to India's other religions. Known as Akbar the Great, the Mughals grew wealthy under his leadership.

TAJ MAHAL

The Mughal Empire was also famed for its magnificent buildings. Emperor Shah Jahan built the Taj Mahal at Agra as a tomb for his favourite wife Mumtaz Mahal, who died in 1631. It took 20 years to complete, needing the labour of 20,000 workers and craftsmen from throughout the Muslim world. Soaring to 73 metres in height and built with white marble inlaid with precious stones, it is regarded as one of the world's most beautiful buildings.

JAMA MASJID, DELHI

THE SHALIMAR GARDEN, LAHORE

KING'S GATE, FATEHPUR SIKRI

1750–1825 THE AGE OF REVOLUTIONS

A series of revolutions swept away long-ruling royal families and shook rulers of colonies in this era. In North America, the United States was established after the British, who ruled colonies there, lost a war against American revolutionaries. Meanwhile in South America the Spanish and Portuguese colonies fought a series of wars to win their independence. In Europe, the French Revolution overthrew the country's king, which was followed by 25 years of war in which the French sent armies into Spain, Germany, Italy, Austria and Russia before they were defeated. European powers, though, continued to explore and sent settlers into new areas, as the British established a colony in Australia.

1781: AMERICAN REVOLUTION

The British surrender to American forces at Yorktown. It marks the end of the American Revolutionary War, which has been fought since 1775 as the colonists try to win independence from Britain. In 1803 the country doubles in size when the United States government buys French land in North America. The new state develops the idea of Manifest Destiny, believing it has a right to acquire all the land between the Atlantic and Pacific oceans.

1769: STEAM ENGINE

Scottish inventor James Watt patents his steam engine, which is then used in new machines to work in mines, mills and factories. It is a key moment in the Industrial Revolution, which changed the way people worked.

1789: FRENCH REVOLUTION

The Storming of the Bastille, a prison in Paris, by a mob marks the start of the French Revolution. It deposes the king and installs a government led by the common people.

1791: HAITIAN REVOLUTION

A revolt breaks out among slaves on French-owned plantations in Haiti. With leaders such as the charismatic Toussaint Louverture, it spreads and eventually the Haitians obtain independence from France.

1799: ROSETTA STONE

The Rosetta Stone, an inscription dating from 196 BC, is discovered by French soldiers in Egypt. It allows scholars finally to decipher ancient Egyptian hieroglyphs.

1810: MEXICAN REVOLUTION

Miguel Hidalgo, a Catholic priest, calls for an uprising against Spanish rule in Mexico. It sparks the Mexican Revolution, which ends with its independence in 1821.

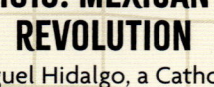

1811: VENEZUELAN INDEPENDENCE

Venezuela becomes independent from Spain after a campaign by Simón Bolívar. Over the next 15 years he and other revolutionary leaders gain the freedom of the whole of Spanish-controlled South America.

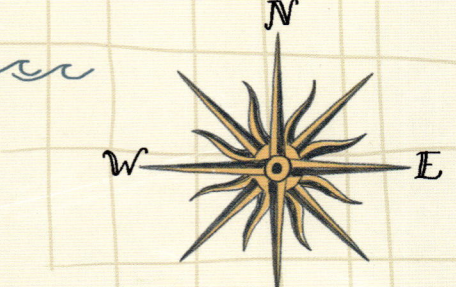

DID YOU KNOW?

Two of the greatest classical music composers in history lived at this time. The Austrian Wolfgang Amadeus Mozart (1756–1791) was a child prodigy who produced more than 600 works. The German Ludwig van Beethoven (1770–1827) composed nine celebrated symphonies, despite losing his hearing.

KEY EVENT: JAMES COOK REACHES AUSTRALIA

While on a voyage in April 1770 in the South Pacific, Captain James Cook spotted the east coast of Australia. Ten days later he landed at Kamay, near modern Sydney. Scientists and artists accompanying Cook recorded many plants and animals they'd never seen before, such as the kangaroo. Cook encountered some of the local people, shooting at two Gweagal men but having peaceful exchanges with the Guugu Yimithirr people. Cook claimed the east coast for Britain, despite Aboriginal Australians having lived there for over 60,000 years. His exploration opened the door for Europeans to settle in Australia.

1812: NAPOLEON RETREATS

French emperor Napoleon has conquered parts of Europe, but when he invades Russia he is forced to retreat. Most of his army deserts or dies from disease, the extreme cold or Russian attacks. It is Napoleon's first major defeat and shatters his reputation for invincibility. He eventually abdicates in 1815.

1796: WHITE LOTUS REBELLION

The White Lotus, a secret religious society, mounts a rebellion in China to try to depose the Qing Dynasty and restore the old Ming Dynasty. It is eventually defeated but much of central China is devastated by bandit groups, resulting in many deaths.

1782: CHAKRI DYNASTY

Rama I, a former military commander, becomes ruler of Thailand, beginning the Chakri Dynasty which still rules today.

1757: BRITISH CONTROL OF INDIA

The British East India Company has been trading from bases in India since the early 1600s. Its army's victory over the Nawab (governor) of Bengal at the Battle of Plassey is the beginning of Britain taking control of Bengal, and then most of India.

1816: ZULU EMPIRE

Shaka Zulu becomes leader of the Zulu kingdom, which expands rapidly until it rules much of modern South Africa. The kingdom remains powerful until it's conquered by the British in 1879.

1788: FIRST FLEET

The First Fleet, eleven ships carrying hundreds of convicts deported from Britain, lands in Australia and founds a colony. It is the first European settlement in Australia. The settlers come into regular conflict with Aboriginal people, as well as introducing them to deadly diseases.

FOCUS ON
THE UNITED STATES
INDEPENDENCE

During the 1600s, Britain established thirteen colonies in eastern North America. Over time the colonists became unhappy that they had few rights, having to pay taxes to Britain even though they could not send representatives to its parliament. When the British imposed even more taxes, some of the colonists protested, and Britain passed oppressive laws which angered them further. In 1775 war broke out as the colonists fought to make their thirteen colonies independent from British rule as the United States of America. This was known as the American Revolution.

THE BOSTON TEA PARTY

One of the main triggers for the American Revolution came when the British government put an extra tax on tea imported into North America. Then, it allowed some British ships to carry tea to the colonies without paying the duty. These measures upset the colonists and in December 1773 a group disguised as Native Americans boarded three British ships and pitched their cargo of tea into the harbour in Boston, Massachusetts. This "Boston Tea Party" caused the British to pass even harsher laws, which made many colonists think they needed to be free of British rule.

THE DECLARATION OF INDEPENDENCE

In 1774 the colonists set up the Continental Congress to organise resistance to the British. By the following year, fighting had broken out between the colonists and the British, and in 1776, the Continental Congress met in Philadelphia where it began drafting a document to declare the thirteen colonies to be an independent nation. This Declaration of Independence was approved on 4 July and the colonies' leaders announced the birth of the United States of America. The anniversary is still a national holiday in the United States. However, the British refused to accept it and the war continued.

THE FOUNDING FATHERS

The United States owed its independence to "Founding Fathers", a group of men who helped the new nation resist the British and decided the way the new country would function. These are just a few of them.

GEORGE WASHINGTON
(1732-1799)
He led the colonists' army and became the first president of the United States in 1789.

BENJAMIN FRANKLIN
(1706-1790)
An inventor, scientist and diplomat, he helped draft the Declaration of Independence and the United States constitution that set out the laws for the country.

JOHN ADAMS
(1735-1826)
He helped negotiate the final peace treaty with Britain and in 1797 he became the second president of the United States.

THOMAS JEFFERSON
(1743-1826)
A lawyer and diplomat, he was the main author of the Declaration of Independence and in 1801 became the third president of the United States.

THE REVOLUTIONARY WAR

From the moment the fighting first broke out in 1775 at Lexington and Concord in Massachusetts, the war between the British and the colonists lasted eight years. Although the British army won some victories, gradually the colonists' Continental Army, led by George Washington, pushed them back. When the French allied with the colonists, Britain lost control of the sea and in 1781 its army surrendered at Yorktown. It was the last major battle of the war, and in 1783 Britain signed a peace treaty with the Americans and recognised the independence of the United States.

1825–1875 UNITY AND REBELLION

The way many countries around the world were ruled changed in different ways during this time. In Japan, the emperors returned and began reforms, while Britain grew its empire in Africa and Asia, leading to conflict with local people and inequality. Civil war almost caused the United States to break apart, but Germany and Italy, which until now had been groups of individual states, united into their own countries. Science continued to advance, with innovations such as the first photography, and the development by Charles Darwin of the theory of evolution.

1845: IRISH FAMINE

A disease destroys the potato crop, a vital part of the diet of people in Ireland, and causes a severe famine (shortage of food). Around a million people die and two million more emigrate, mainly to the USA.

IRELAND ●

GERMANY ●

1826: FIRST PHOTO

Nicéphore Niépce takes the first ever photograph, of the street outside his studio in France, using a camera obscura. It takes eight hours for the photo to develop.

1863: AMERICAN CIVIL WAR

Since 1861 the American Civil War has been fought over the issue of slavery, between the Union and the southern states who have broken away from the Union and call themselves the Confederacy. Union states' victory at the Battle of Gettysburg in 1863 marks a turning point and two years later the Confederacy is defeated and slavery is abolished all over the USA, though freed former slaves still face serious discrimination.

1847: LIBERIAN INDEPENDENCE

Liberia, founded in 1821 as a settlement for free African Americans and former slaves, becomes fully independent. It is one of only two countries in Africa (with Ethiopia) to escape European colonisation.

1864: WAR OF THE TRIPLE ALLIANCE

The War of the Triple Alliance breaks out between Paraguay and its neighbours Uruguay, Brazil and Argentina. The war is devastating for Paraguay, which loses territory and around 60 per cent of its population, one of the worst casualty rates in history.

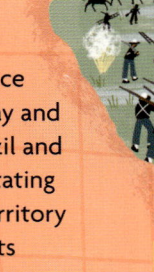

DID YOU KNOW?

In 1837 the English inventor Charles Babbage designed the Analytical Engine, a mechanical calculating machine. Although it is thought of as the first computer, it was so complex that the engineering of the time couldn't actually build it. Ada Lovelace wrote a set of instructions for the Analytical Engine, becoming the world's first computer programmer.

KEY EVENT: THEORY OF EVOLUTION

It was 1859 when the English scientist Charles Darwin published a theory that shocked many people and challenged Christian beliefs. His theory of evolution stated that living creatures change over time through natural selection, which means animals that are best suited to their environment survive longer and have more young. He based much of his work on observations of birds and tortoises made on a voyage to the Galapagos Islands in 1835.

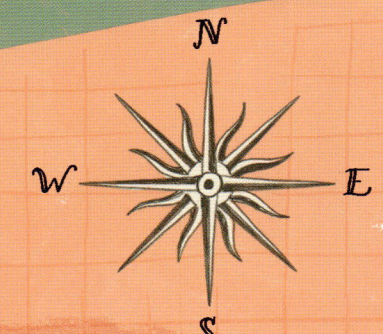

1868: MEIJI RESTORATION

The last Tokugawa shogun is overthrown and Emperor Meiji Tenno takes power in Japan. This begins the Meiji Restoration, when the country opens up to Europe and abolishes the power of the samurai.

1853: CRIMEAN WAR

The Crimean War breaks out between the Ottoman Empire and Russia. Britain and France join in on the side of the Ottomans. It is the first time photography is used to record a war and the beginning of modern nursing, after Florence Nightingale's work in a military hospital dramatically reduces deaths among soldiers there. By 1856 Russia is defeated.

1871: UNIFICATION

Wilhelm I of Prussia declares himself emperor of Germany, completing the process of unifying the German states. Italy is also unified this year after a military campaign led by the revolutionary Giuseppe Garibaldi.

JAPAN

1839: OPIUM WAR

The First Opium War breaks out between Britain and China. British merchants make huge profits selling the drug opium to China, causing millions of Chinese people to become addicted to it. China's efforts to stop the trade lead to naval battles. The British are victorious and gain possession of Hong Kong, which they keep control of until 1997.

1857: INDIAN REBELLION

An uprising breaks out among Indian soldiers (sepoys) in the British East India Company army. The rebellion is defeated after much violence, the last Mughal emperor is exiled and the British government takes control of India.

1840: BRITISH TREATY

Maori chiefs agree to the Treaty of Waitangi, made by the British government. It means Britain can claim New Zealand as a colony, but promises Maori chiefs can keep control over their lands.

1835: GREAT TREK

Dutch-speaking settlers seeking to escape British rule in Cape Colony (in modern South Africa) begin a "Great Trek" northwards across Africa. They clash with the Zulu but found their own independent states there.

1875–1922 THE WORLD AT WAR

Several great empires ended in this period. The First World War weakened European countries, while the Russian Empire was taken over by a communist revolution, where the government took control of all the land and factories. In China, the last emperor was overthrown after a series of revolts, including the Boxer Rebellion, which protested against foreign influence in the country.

1876: FIRST TELEPHONE CALL

Alexander Graham Bell, the inventor of the telephone, makes the first ever call to his assistant Thomas Watson, next door in their Boston Laboratory, saying, "Mr Watson, come here, I want to see you."

1921: BRITISH EMPIRE

The British Empire becomes the largest empire of all time, ruling almost a quarter of land in the world. However independence movements are growing, as Ireland leaves the empire and other colonies protest British rule.

1876: BATTLE OF THE LITTLE BIGHORN

The American-Indian Wars of the 1800s are fought between Native Americans and settlers who had been seizing their land. At the Battle of the Little Bighorn, Cheyenne and Lakota Sioux warriors led by Sitting Bull defeat the US army, but it is a rare Native American victory and by 1890 they are defeated and forced to live in reservations, where they find it hard to keep their cultural traditions.

1892: ELLIS ISLAND

The United States immigration processing centre at Ellis Island opens in New York harbour. During its years of operation (to 1954), more than twelve million migrants arrive here, often fleeing political persecution or poor living conditions. They arrive by boat for inspection before they are allowed to enter the country.

1914: FIRST WORLD WAR

A Serbian revolutionary assassinates the Austrian Archduke Franz Ferdinand. European powers line up behind either Serbia or Austria-Hungary, leading to the outbreak of the First World War, which lasts four years and costs around twenty million lives.

1897: END OF BENIN

A British expedition attacks and captures Benin city to end the kingdom of Benin. The British loot Benin treasures including bronze plaques from the palace. Most areas of Africa are colonised by European powers by 1900.

DID YOU KNOW?

The first ever powered flight was made by the American Wright brothers on 17 December 1903. Their aeroplane was made of fabric and wood and stayed off the ground for just 12 seconds, travelling around 40 metres. It was the beginning of the age of aviation.

1911: SOUTH POLE EXPEDITION

A Norwegian expedition led by Roald Amundsen becomes the first ever to reach the South Pole, beating Robert Scott's British team by five weeks.

KEY EVENT: BOXER REBELLION

Many people in China were unhappy at the growing interference of Europeans, who controlled ports along China's coast. Some in the Chinese government encouraged a secret society called the "Righteous and Harmonious Fists" (also known as Boxers), who were dedicated to expelling the foreigners, to attack the capital Beijing in 1900. The Boxers captured the city and besieged foreign embassies there, and an expedition sent by countries including Japan, Russia, Britain, the United States and France invaded China to rescue their diplomats. The Chinese government was forced to sign a peace agreement with the foreign powers, agreeing to pay a huge sum in compensation. This only caused more Chinese people to feel that the emperors couldn't defend China, and that the system needed to change.

1917: RUSSIAN REVOLUTION

A revolution overthrows the Russian Tsar Nicholas II, and a communist group (who believe private ownership should be abolished, and land and wealth shared out equally by the government) led by Vladimir Lenin take over. After a civil war they establish the Union of Soviet Socialist Republics (USSR) in 1922.

1911: CHINESE REVOLUTION

A rebellion against the Qing Dynasty ends 2,100 years of emperors ruling in China. Many traditional practices, such as the Manchu queue (plait), are abandoned. A government is formed to rule over the new Republic of China.

1919: INDEPENDENCE PROTESTS

A British commander in Amritsar orders his troops to fire on a crowd of unarmed Indian protesters, killing hundreds. Support for the Indian independence movement led by Mahatma Gandhi rises, and he leads peaceful protests to try to persuade the British to leave India.

1896: ETHIOPIA INDEPENDENT

Emperor Menelik II of Ethiopia defeats an invading Italian army at the Battle of Adwa, meaning the country remains one of only two (with Liberia) in Africa to escape European colonisation.

1893: VOTES FOR WOMEN

Women in New Zealand become the first to be allowed to vote in elections, after a campaign by women known as suffragists, such as Kate Sheppard.

FOCUS ON
THE FIRST WORLD WAR
TRENCH WARFARE

The First World War broke out in August 1914. After a young Serbian killed an Austrian archduke, Germany supported Austria-Hungary (known as the Central Powers), but Russia, France, Britain and Italy supported Serbia (known as the Allies). Soon fighting broke out between the two sides in Europe, the Middle East and East Africa. In an area of Europe known as the Western Front, in Belgium and France, they both dug long systems of trenches to make it difficult for the other side to attack. Attempts to do so cost hundreds of thousands of soldiers' lives over the course of the war.

THE TRENCHES

The trenches were around two metres wide and three metres deep, so soldiers could stand in them without exposing themselves to enemy fire. Sandbags and barbed wire gave the trenches extra protection and they were often built in a zigzag pattern to make them harder to attack. Life in the trenches was difficult and unhealthy: the damp ground caused infections and many soldiers had to have feet or toes amputated, or died from exposure to the cold.

KEY DATES

Many battles were fought during the First World War, and by its end around 10 million soldiers had died. These are some of the most important moments in the war.

SEPTEMBER 1914
BATTLE OF THE MARNE

The German army almost defeats the French at the start of the war, but the French hold firm. It means the war will not be over quickly.

JULY 1916
BATTLE OF THE SOMME

Three million soldiers take part in the war's largest battle with more than a million casualties.

FIGHTING

For most of the time soldiers waited in the trenches, patrolling or making repairs. Every so often, generals ordered an attack, and the soldiers left their trench to try to take the enemy trench opposite. This meant they had to cross the wide space in between, called no man's land, and cut through barbed wire and other obstacles while under fire from enemy machine-guns. Casualties were very high during such attacks and they normally gained very little ground.

NEW WEAPONS

The two sides invented new weapons which they thought might allow them to capture enemy trenches more easily. In 1916 the British developed the tank, a heavily armoured vehicle on tracks which could cross muddy ground and protected soldiers from machine-gun fire. The early versions, though, were unreliable and often broke down.

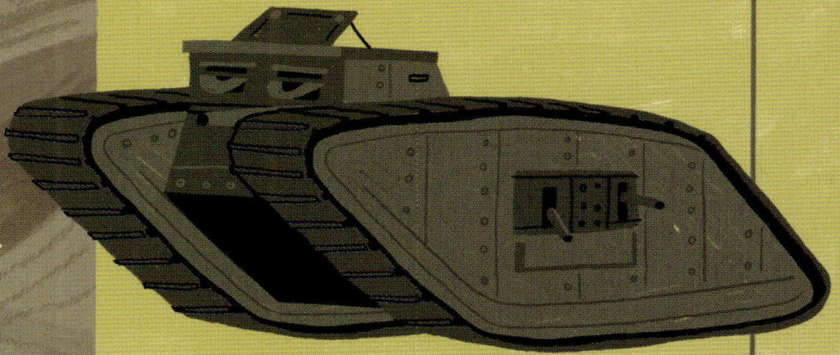

The armies also created poison gas, which was hugely painful and sometimes deadly when breathed in. Towards the end of the war aeroplanes were used over the battlefield, first to spy and make maps, and then to drop bombs on enemy trenches and vehicles. In 1918, after four years of fighting, the Allies broke through and the war ended.

APRIL 1917

USA JOINS WAR

When the United States joins the Allies after German attacks on American ships, its army tips the balance against the Germans.

NOVEMBER 1918

ARMISTICE

After its forces are pushed back, Germany asks for peace and signs an armistice ending the war.

WAR OVER

1922–1945 WAR AND PEACE

After the First World War, people hoped for a return to peace and wealth, but their dreams were shattered by the Great Depression, when trade between countries dried up and millions lost their jobs. This led many to vote for extreme political parties who promised a better life. In Germany the National Socialists (Nazis) came to power under Adolf Hitler. His armies marched into parts of Europe that Germany claimed should belong to it, leading to the outbreak of the Second World War, during which large parts of Europe and Asia were devastated. Meanwhile the Nazis persecuted Jewish people, first in Germany and then across Europe.

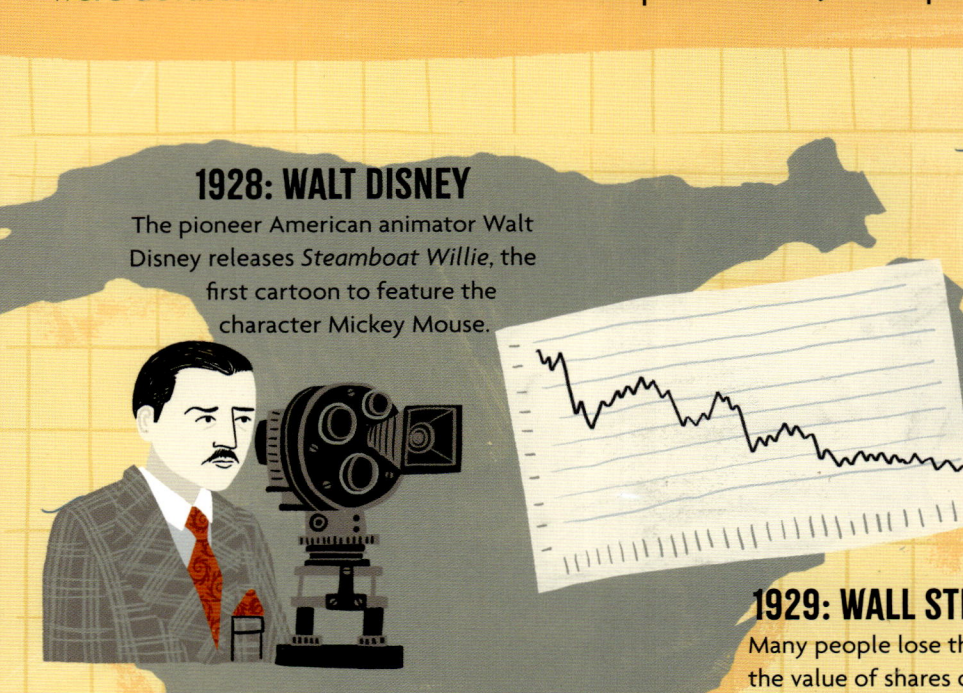

1928: WALT DISNEY
The pioneer American animator Walt Disney releases *Steamboat Willie*, the first cartoon to feature the character Mickey Mouse.

1922: IRISH CIVIL WAR
A civil war breaks out between the Irish government and people opposed to the terms of the treaty that has made the south of Ireland independent from the United Kingdom. The government claims victory but divisions remain.

IRELAND

SPAIN

1929: WALL STREET CRASH
Many people lose their savings after the value of shares on the New York Stock Market dramatically drops in the Wall Street Crash. Economies collapse and unemployment rises worldwide in what is known as the Great Depression.

1936: SPANISH CIVIL WAR
General Francisco Franco mounts an army rebellion against the Spanish government, sparking a civil war. Civilians, including women, and volunteers from abroad join the fighting as cities become battlefields. Franco captures Madrid in 1939 and becomes dicatator of Spain until his death in 1975.

DID YOU KNOW?
Albert Einstein, one of the most famous scientists of all time, received the Nobel Prize in Physics in 1922. His theory of relativity explained how space, time and gravity all influence each other to create the universe, and his energy equation $e=mc^2$ is the most famous equation of all time.

1930: VARGAS ERA
Getúlio Vargas leads a revolt and takes power in Brazil. He rules as a dictator from 1937, suppressing all opposition. He also introduces reforms aimed to raise workers' wages and encourage industry.

KEY EVENT: KRISTALLNACHT

After he came to power in 1934, Adolf Hitler's measures against German Jews became increasingly harsh. Jewish students were not allowed to study in universities and Jewish-owned businesses were confiscated. In November 1938 the Nazi party organised a series of attacks against Jewish businesses and places of worship. Dozens of Jewish people were killed and 30,000 were arrested and imprisoned in concentration camps, where hundreds of them died. It was called Kristallnacht ("crystal night") because of the broken glass that littered the streets after the attacks. During the Second World War, the Nazis killed six million Jewish people in what is known as the Holocaust.

1939: SECOND WORLD WAR

German troops invade Poland, and when Britain and France respond by declaring war on Germany, the Second World War begins. The biggest war in history, it lasts six years and costs over 70 million lives.

1928: FIVE-YEAR PLAN

Joseph Stalin takes control of the USSR and establishes a series of Five-Year Plans to modernise the country and improve industry. He seizes peasants' land and millions die during famines. Stalin has opponents executed.

1937: JAPAN INVADES CHINA

Japan launches an attack on eastern China. Its army seizes the capital Nanking and unleashes brutal attacks on its population, killing at least 100,000 civilians.

1930: LAST EMPEROR

Haile Selassie becomes emperor of Ethiopia, the last of a line of rulers that dates back 700 years. He is forced to leave his country for five years when the Italians invade in 1936, and is overthrown in 1974 after a severe famine.

1930: GANDHI'S SALT MARCH

Mahatma Gandhi continues his non-violent campaign against British rule in India, and leads a "Salt March" to gather salt at the seashore (an act illegal under British rule). Gandhi is arrested but it gets international attention, and he continues to campaign for Indian independence (which is achieved in 1947).

1934: LONG MARCH

A civil war has been fought in China between the government and the communist party since 1927. In 1934 the communists, led by Mao Zedong, are forced to retreat from their headquarters in the south on a "Long March", 8,000 kilometres across the country. Thousands die, but the rest reach safety in northern China after a year.

AUSTRALIA

1930: FEMALE SOLO FLIGHT

Amy Johnson becomes the first woman to make a solo flight from Britain to Australia. It takes her nineteen days.

FOCUS ON
THE SECOND WORLD WAR
AIR RAIDS

The fighting in the Second World War (1939–1945) affected the whole of Europe, North Africa, East and South East Asia, the Pacific Islands and the Atlantic Ocean. Although there had been a few air raids during the First World War, it was only now that bombs were dropped in large numbers on cities and industrial sites in countries including Britain, the USSR, China and Germany. The idea was to cause fear and damage and to force surrender. German bomber planes attacked many British cities in 1940–1941, and towards the end of the war British and American air raids caused enormous damage to German cities such as Dresden, killing hundreds of thousands of civilians. The countries being attacked tried to defend themselves with fighter aircraft and anti-aircraft guns.

THE BLITZ

In September 1940, having failed to defeat the British air force, the German air force (known as the Luftwaffe) turned to bombing British cities instead. In this wave of attacks, called the Blitz, London suffered German air raids every night for almost two months. Many other British cities were attacked including Liverpool, Coventry, Swansea, Belfast and Glasgow, where the raids also targeted shipyards. Over 43,000 people were killed, and tens of thousands of buildings were damaged, including the Houses of Parliament. The Blitz ended in May 1941. Later in the war, the British and Americans increased their air raids on German cities, hoping to end the fighting by destroying German morale. Hundreds of thousands of civilians were killed.

BLITZ BOMBING GOES ON ALL NIGHT

KEY DATES

The Second World War involved countries in every part of the world. It was the deadliest conflict in history, with over 70 million people estimated to have died. Here are some of the key events.

September 1939 – War breaks out after Germany invades Poland.

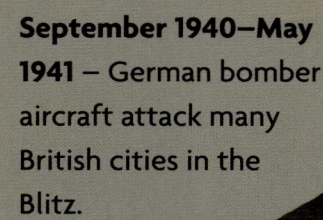

September 1940–May 1941 – German bomber aircraft attack many British cities in the Blitz.

June 1941 – Germany invades the Soviet Union, but the attack ends in defeat for the Germans.

EVACUATION

To protect civilians, governments closed schools and evacuated children from towns and cities to the countryside. During raids, people were warned of the attacks by air-raid sirens and protected themselves in reinforced air-raid shelters. In London people slept underground on Tube station platforms. Strict laws were passed in Britain that people had to cover their windows in blackout curtains to stop light escaping and make it harder for German bombers to see their targets.

ATOMIC BOMBS

During the war, the United States developed atomic weapons, which were far more powerful than normal bombs. In August 1945 the American air force dropped atomic bombs on the Japanese cities of Nagasaki and Hiroshima. It's estimated over 200,000 Japanese civilians were killed: many died from the effects of the radiation released by the explosions. Japan surrendered soon afterwards, ending the Second World War.

August 1945 — The United States drops atomic bombs on Japan, ending the war in the Pacific.

December 1941 — The United States joins the war after the Japanese attack on its Pearl Harbor naval base.

February 1945 — Britain and America bomb the German city of Dresden, killing 25,000 civilians.

May 1945 — The Russians capture Berlin and Germany surrenders, ending the war in Europe.

1953: QUEEN ELIZABETH II

Elizabeth II is crowned as Queen of the United Kingdom. Her coronation leads to a surge in people buying televisions, which were previously uncommon, to watch the ceremony. She will become the country's longest-reigning monarch.

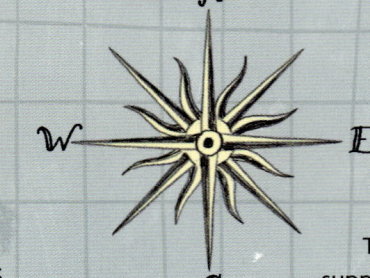

UNITED KINGDOM ●   BERLIN ●

1955: CIVIL RIGHTS MOVEMENT

Rosa Parks is arrested after she refuses to move to seats allocated to black people at the back of a bus in Alabama. In 1956 the US Supreme Court rules that restricting where black people can sit is illegal – an important moment in their fight for equal rights and against segregation (the idea that black people should not be allowed to use the same facilities, schools and housing as white people).

1948: BERLIN BLOCKADE

The Soviet Union cuts off food and medicine supplies to West Berlin, which is allocated to the British, French and Americans after the Second World War. These countries send planes to drop over two million tonnes of supplies into West Berlin and save the city from Soviet occupation.

● CUBA

1959: CUBAN REVOLUTION

Fidel Castro overthrows the government in Cuba, which is supported by the USA. He installs a communist government, and remains president until 2008. Many Cubans flee communist rule and settle in the United States.

1946: PRESIDENT PERÓN

Juan Perón becomes President of Argentina. He and his wife Eva (nicknamed Evita) are at first highly popular with poorer workers, but Eva dies in 1952 and Juan loses support and is exiled in 1955.

1957: GHANA INDEPENDENCE

Ghana becomes independent, with Kwame Nkrumah as its first president. It is the first of Britain's sub-Saharan African colonies to gain independence.

1948: APARTHEID

The National Party government in South Africa introduces apartheid, where races are separated from each other. Black South Africans suffer severe discrimination, including only being allowed to live in certain areas.

1945–1960 DAWN OF A NEW WORLD

The end of the Second World War brought fresh problems. The Soviet Union and its allies, which believed in the political system of communism, were opposed by the United States and nations friendly to it, who supported democracy. This led to the Cold War: the USA and the Soviet Union never fought each other directly, but supported different sides in a series of wars. Meanwhile, many countries in Africa and Asia fought for and won their independence, as European countries struggled to find the money or energy to keep their large empires.

KEY EVENT: PARTITION

After the British government decided that it could no longer keep control of India, it granted independence in 1947, but partitioned the country into two sections: a Muslim-majority Pakistan in the north-west and part of the north-east; and a Hindu-majority India in the rest. Millions of Hindus and Muslims found themselves on the wrong side of this partition and violence broke out in many places. Millions of displaced people were forced to migrate, walking or taking overcrowded trains. Over a million people were killed and tensions and conflict caused by the partition have continued to the present day.

1958: GREAT LEAP FORWARD

The communist party wins the Chinese Civil War and its leader, Mao Zedong, announces the creation of the People's Republic of China in 1949. In 1958 Mao introduces the "Great Leap Forward", in an effort to increase industrial production and improve farming. It causes a famine in which 45 million people die.

ISRAEL ●

1957: FIRST DOG IN SPACE

The dog Laika becomes the first animal to reach space, when she is sent into orbit by the Soviet Union in their Sputnik 2 spacecraft. The craft is not designed to return, and so Laika does not survive.

1950: KOREAN WAR

Communist North Korea invades its neighbour South Korea, beginning the Korean War. Soldiers from the USA join the war on the side of South Korea, while China supports the North. Millions are killed until, after three years, a ceasefire is called.

1948: ISRAEL INDEPENDENCE

The State of Israel is proclaimed by Jewish leader David Ben-Gurion, sparking a war with its Arab neighbours. Around 700,000 Palestinian Arabs flee or are expelled from their homes.

1953: MOUNT EVEREST

New Zealander Edmund Hillary and Nepalese Sherpa Tenzing Norgay become the first people to succesfully climb Mount Everest, the world's highest mountain at 8,849 metres.

1954: VIETNAM WAR

Ho Chi Minh establishes a communist republic in North Vietnam after throwing off French rule. He invades South Vietnam in 1959, beginning the Vietnam War. The US sends support for the South.

NET NIE·BLANKES NON EUROPEANS ONLY | NET BLANKES. EUROPEANS ONLY

1960-1974 NEW HORIZONS

The Cold War continued as the United States and Soviet Union tried to increase their influence as world superpowers. Crises over Berlin and Cuba nearly led to actual war between them, but starting a war with nuclear weapons was too dangerous for either side. Even science was touched by superpower rivalry as the two nations raced to become the first to send a man into space, and then to place one on the Moon.

1972: THE TROUBLES

Thirteen people are killed after British soldiers fire on Catholic unarmed demonstrators in Northern Ireland. It is one of the worst incidents in "The Troubles", a period of violence and unrest between those who want Northern Ireland to stay part of the United Kingdom, and those who want a united Ireland.

1974: WATERGATE SCANDAL

Richard Nixon becomes the first US president to resign. He is forced to quit after the Watergate scandal, when it is found he has secretly taped conversations in an attempt to cover up a break-in at the headquarters of the opposition Democratic Party.

1962: CUBAN MISSILE CRISIS

The US discovers the Soviet Union is building launch sites for nuclear missiles on Cuba. For thirteen days the world stands on the brink of a nuclear war, before the Soviet Union agrees to withdraw them.

N
W · E
S

1973: CHILEAN COUP

Chile's president, Salvador Allende, is overthrown by the army and killed by Augusto Pinochet, the army chief, who is supported by the United States and becomes dictator of the country. He clamps down on former Allende supporters, killing 3,000 of them. Many of the victims are never found.

DID YOU KNOW?

One of the most important moments in the American civil rights movement took place on 28 August 1963. Around 250,000 people marched in Washington DC as Martin Luther King made his famous "I have a dream" speech, setting out his vision of equality for all Americans. In the following years equal rights laws were introduced, but King was assassinated in 1968.

KEY EVENT: FIRST MAN ON THE MOON

When the Soviet Union sent the first man into space in 1961, it was a blow to the United States' hopes of being the pioneers of space travel. So in the same year President Kennedy announced that America would send the first man to the Moon before 1970. This accelerated the "space race" between the two countries. The US space agency NASA worked hard to develop technology and in July 1969 the Apollo 11 mission launched from Cape Canaveral, Florida. On 21 July its commander, Neil Armstrong, opened the hatch of the lunar lander and took the first step on the Moon, announcing "one small step for [a] man, one giant leap for mankind".

1961: BERLIN WALL

The communist government of East Germany builds a wall in Berlin to stop thousands of its citizens fleeing to the West.

1961: FIRST MAN IN SPACE

The Soviet Union's Yuri Gagarin becomes the first man in space. He completes a single orbit of the Earth in the Vostok 1 capsule.

1966: CULTURAL REVOLUTION

Chairman Mao Zedong launches the Cultural Revolution, encouraging students to attack symbols of traditional China, including temples and universities. He issues the Little Red Book to inspire them with his quotes. Many cities descend into chaos and hundreds of thousands of people die over the next decade.

CHINA

1973: YOM KIPPUR WAR

A group of Arab states invades Israel during the Jewish holiday of Yom Kippur to try to capture territory won by Israel in the 1967 Six Days War. The war lasts less than a month but leads to an increase in oil prices and a global economic crisis.

VIETNAM

1973: USA LEAVES VIETNAM

The United States starts to pull its troops out of Vietnam, ending its part in the Vietnam War. It has become increasingly involved in the war, sending troops to support the South and using helicopters to take them into battlefields. After two more years of fighting, communist forces capture the South and the country is unified.

1964: NELSON MANDELA JAILED

Nelson Mandela and other members of the African National Congress, a group opposed to apartheid in South Africa, are jailed for life for acts of sabotage against the government.

1975 –1989 A NEW WORLD ORDER

The Cold War dominated world events in this period – but it wouldn't for much longer. Although some communist leaders took power in South East Asia, the Soviet Union itself was struggling and could no longer afford to support other communist countries. By 1989 protests were breaking out in eastern European countries run by governments that supported the Soviet Union. One of the most famous was in Germany, where the Berlin Wall, built to divide the communist East Germany from the West, was knocked down.

1975: THE AGE OF COMPUTERS

The age of computers begins as Microsoft is founded in the USA by Bill Gates and Paul Allen. It provides software for computer manufacturers, and is hugely important in making computers part of people's everyday lives in the following years. In 1977 the world's first personal computers become widely available, such as the Apple II.

KEY EVENT:
THE FALL OF THE BERLIN WALL

The Berlin Wall had stood for nearly 30 years when, on 9 November 1989, television in East Germany announced that the border with West Germany was about to open. This came after huge protests against the communist government, and so tens of thousands of East Germans passed through checkpoints along the Berlin Wall into the West, a journey previously forbidden to them. People used hammers and pickaxes to knock away chunks of the wall. The East German government's authority was shattered and a year later East and West Germany were reunited into a single country.

1978: WORLD CUP

Argentina hosts the football World Cup for the first time, and its team wins for the first time. They win again in 1986, but controversially their star player Diego Maradona scores a goal with his hand, claiming he is helped by the "hand of God".

1982: FALKLANDS WAR

War breaks out between Britain and Argentina, after Argentina invades the British-held Falkland Islands, claiming they own them. The British send warships and retake the islands two months later.

F170

1986: CHERNOBYL DISASTER

An accident at the Chernobyl nuclear power station in Ukraine sends a cloud of radioactive material drifting over Europe. It is the worst disaster in the history of nuclear power. Hundreds of people suffer from radiation sickness, and some are killed.

1985: MIKHAIL GORBACHEV

Mikhail Gorbachev becomes leader of the Soviet Union. He launches policies to reverse years of economic and industrial decline and modernise the country.

1989: TIANANMEN SQUARE PROTESTS

Chinese authorities send the army to stop a pro-democracy demonstration in Tiananmen Square, Bejing. It is estimated that hundreds of unarmed protestors are killed. A man blocking the path of the tanks becomes a famous image of the event.

IRAN

1979: IRANIAN REVOLUTION

The Muslim leader Ayatollah Khomeini founds an Islamic Republic in Iran, which imposes a strict interpretation of Islamic law.

1975: KHMER ROUGE

The Khmer Rouge, a radical communist group led by Pol Pot, moves the population of Cambodia's capital city to the countryside to work on farms and reject money and religion. Over the next four years, two million Cambodians are executed, or die from starvation or disease. In 1979 Vietnam invades and overthrows the Khmer Rouge.

1984: ETHIOPIAN FAMINE

A drought hits Ethiopia, leading to a serious famine in which a million people die. Musicians in Britain, Ireland and the USA release singles and organise the Live Aid concert to raise money for famine relief.

1980: ZIMBABWE INDEPENDENCE

Following a civil war, Zimbabwe is declared independent and given a new flag. The country has previously been a British colony known as Rhodesia, whose prime minister Ian Smith tried to make it independent as a white-ruled country. Robert Mugabe is elected as its first prime minister.

DID YOU KNOW?

The Rubik's cube puzzle became a huge sensation during this period. It was invented by the Hungarian professor Erno Rubik in 1974 and released worldwide in 1980. It is a cube split up into 27 smaller cubes with coloured faces, which are rotated until all the colours on each side of the larger cube match. There are 43 billion billion possible combinations for the cube. Fortunately, it can be solved and it sold millions during the 1980s.

57

1990-2001 THE MODERN WORLD

By now, anti-communist protests and uprisings had brought an end to the Cold War. The United States was left in a powerful position, but this did not bring peace to the world. With the danger of nuclear war between the superpowers gone, several smaller conflicts broke out. Meanwhile other countries, particularly China, grew strong as they invested in the new technology that was starting to change the world, such as mobile phones and the internet.

KEY EVENT: BIRTH OF THE INTERNET

In 1990 the British computer scientist Tim Berners Lee created the first ever web browser, which made viewing web pages possible. The following year he put up the world's first website that could be accessed by anyone. Scientists had been developing the internet since the 1960s, but this was the beginning of its use by the public. In the years that followed it transformed how people worldwide communicated, shopped, studied and more. By 2019 there were an estimated 1.7 billion websites and 4.3 billion people with internet access.

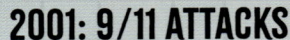

1998: PEACE DEAL

The Good Friday Agreement brings an end to The Troubles, the decades of violence between groups who disagree about Northern Ireland being part of the United Kingdom. The agreement means Catholics and Protestants will share power.

2001: 9/11 ATTACKS

Terrorists from the Al-Qaeda Islamic extremist group hijack aeroplanes in the United States, flying two of them into the World Trade Center twin towers in New York, and a third into the Pentagon building in Washington DC. Almost 3,000 people are killed, which leads US President George Bush to announce a "War on Terror".

1992: GLOBAL WARMING

The first Earth Summit is held in Rio de Janeiro, Brazil, bringing together countries to try to solve environmental issues that are too complicated for any one nation. This includes global warming, which is the process of the Earth getting hotter because of human activity and pollution. Later summits lead to countries signing the Kyoto Protocol and Paris Agreement to try to slow down climate change.

DID YOU KNOW?

In the early 1990s very few people owned a mobile phone. But during this period the technology quickly improved, phones got smaller and cheaper and soon they were everywhere, with manufacturers selling hundreds of millions of handsets worldwide. In 2001 the world's first 3G phone service, which allowed easy mobile internet use, was launched in Japan.

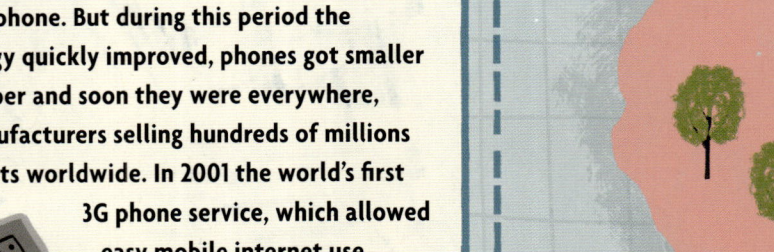

1996: FIRST CLONE

Dolly the sheep becomes the first mammal to be cloned by growing a new animal from a cell taken from an adult sheep in Scotland.

SCOTLAND

1992: BOSNIAN WAR

Civil war breaks out in Bosnia-Herzegovina after it declares independence from Yugoslavia. Fighting between Serbs and Bosnian Muslims and Croats engulfs the country. The capital Sarajevo suffers a brutal siege by Serbs. Eventually a 1995 peace deal divides the country into separate areas.

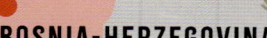

BOSNIA-HERZEGOVINA

1991: END OF THE SOVIET UNION

Regions of the Soviet Union start claiming their independence after revolutions against communist rule. When Mikhail Gorbachev resigns as president the Soviet Union dissolves into 15 separate countries, including Russia.

1992: EUROPEAN UNION

The Maastricht Treaty is signed to create the European Union, a group of countries that work together on major issues. The EU sets up the Single European Market, so they can trade more easily with each other.

KUWAIT

1990: GULF WAR

The Iraqi dictator Saddam Hussein invades Kuwait, which he claims to be part of Iraq. A group of countries including the USA, UK and Saudi Arabia launches Operation Desert Storm in 1991, sending bomber planes followed by troops. They succeed in freeing Kuwait, but a ban on trade and other tensions between Iraq and other countries leads to another war in 2003.

1994: RWANDAN GENOCIDE

Violence breaks out in Rwanda after the president is assassinated. Many people from the Hutu ethnic group engage in mass killings of Tutsi people. 800,000 people are killed over 100 days.

1994: NELSON MANDELA ELECTED

Nelson Mandela is elected president of South Africa in the country's first elections open to people of all races. He was released from prison after 27 years in 1990 as the policy of apartheid came to an end.

59

HOW HISTORY HAPPENS NOW

Today's world is a vastly more connected place than it was in the past. Whereas in ancient times it might have taken years to make a journey between countries and some parts of the world were not even in contact, in the 21st century we can fly to the other side of the globe in less than a day, and information travels in a fraction of a second.

21ST CENTURY

SOCIAL MEDIA AND SMARTPHONES

Social media sites and smartphones are new inventions: Facebook was created in 2004, the first iPhone was launched in 2007 and even the internet as we know it is only about 30 years old. These all allow us to find information and share it very quickly, but they also mean that misinformation, some of it made up to be deliberately harmful, can spread rapidly.

GLOBAL FINANCIAL CRISIS

In 2008 a financial crisis which began in the United States, when many people could not repay housing loans, threatened to cause many banks to become bankrupt. If this had happened, the systems which allowed countries to trade with each other might have collapsed, leading to mass unemployment. World leaders acted together to restore confidence in the system and reduce the damage to the global economy. Even so, events in one country can still quickly cause the values of stock markets or currencies in another to fall, meaning governments have to be more alert than ever to prevent more disasters.

As well as creating huge opportunities for sharing knowledge and working together to solve problems such as climate change, this presents dangers. A problem in one country can spread rapidly to affect the whole world, and no one country alone can solve the world's greatest challenges. Yet scientific advances, such as sequencing (working out) the human genome (DNA), and huge increases in computing power mean we have far more powerful tools to help our world than we had even twenty years ago. These are just a few of the issues that are shaping how history happens now.

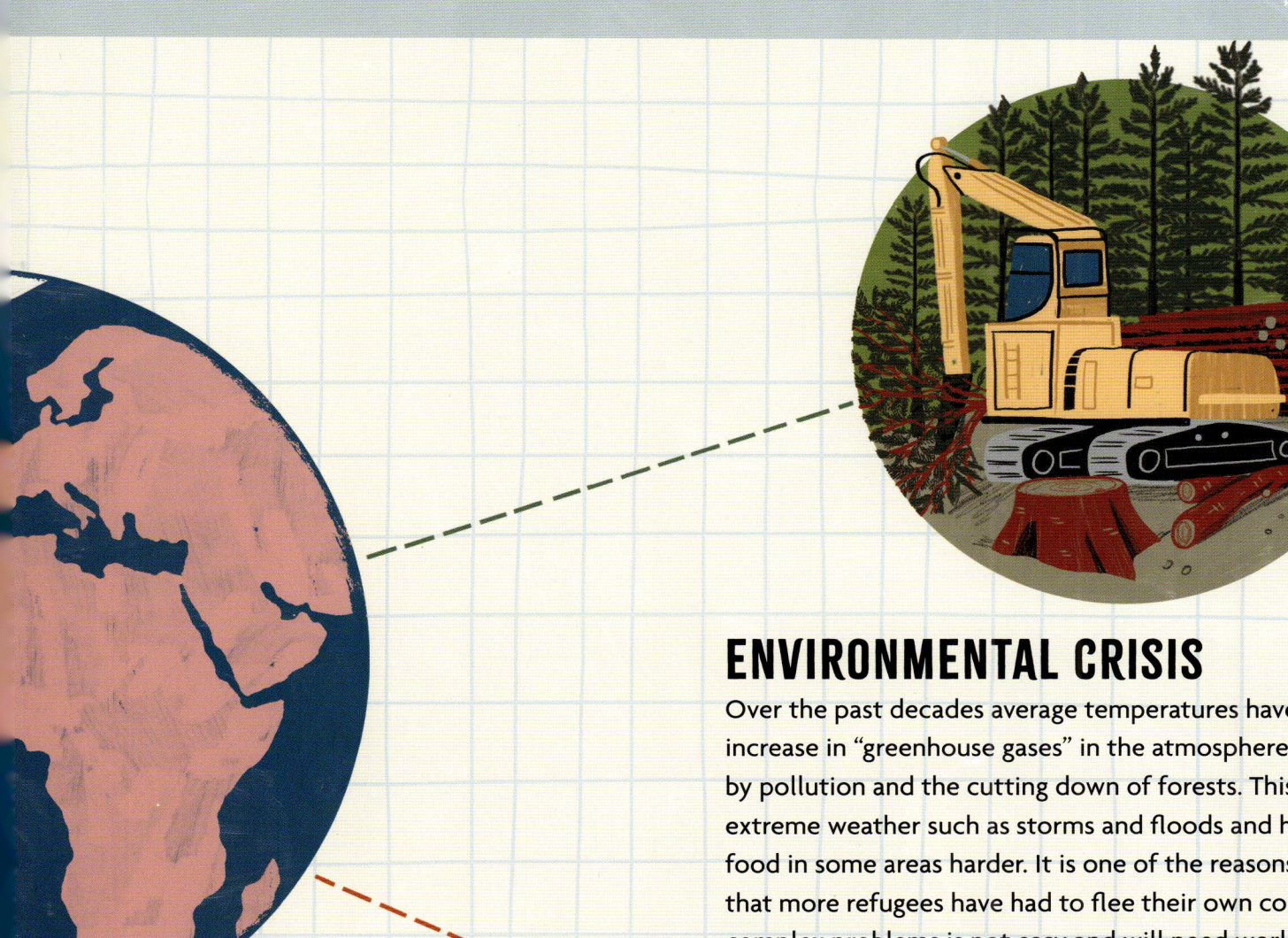

ENVIRONMENTAL CRISIS

Over the past decades average temperatures have risen, caused by an increase in "greenhouse gases" in the atmosphere, which are produced by pollution and the cutting down of forests. This has led to more extreme weather such as storms and floods and has made growing food in some areas harder. It is one of the reasons, together with wars, that more refugees have had to flee their own countries. Solving these complex problems is not easy and will need world leaders to work together for many years.

CORONAVIRUS

International travel has become easier and quicker than ever. The busiest airports have more than 100 million travellers a year. This also means that diseases can spread more quickly than before. In late 2019 the coronavirus pandemic was first detected in one city in China and spread within a few months to affect almost every country in the world. It caused millions of deaths, but also started an international effort to find a vaccine against the virus.

INDEX

NOTE ON MAPS AND DATES

There are many ways to show the world in maps and many systems of dates to describe when events took place. Maps in the Middle Ages often showed Jerusalem at the centre, and modern maps produced in the United States might show North America in the middle, while those from China place East Asia at the centre. In this book we have used maps which have Europe in the middle, but this does not mean that Europe is most important in world history.

The system of dates has changed over time and in different places. The ancient Maya used a calendar which had its first year in 3114 BC, and the modern Islamic calendar began in AD 622. In this book we have used the AD/BC system of dates, which is the most widely used system. It was first used by the Christian Church and that is why it dates the start of the calendar to the traditional date of the birth of Jesus Christ. BC stands for dates "Before Christ" and AD for dates "Anno Domini", which is Latin for "in the year of the Lord" and means after Christ was born. Sometimes these dates are also given as BCE and CE (for "before common era" and "common era").

Sometimes you'll see "c." before a date, like c. 300 BC. The "c" stands for "circa", which is Latin for "about", and means that nobody is quite sure of the exact date of that event, but we know it took place somewhere around that year.